CREATE AN ADHD-FRIENDLY

Personal Owner's Manual

by Patty Blinderman, PCC, PCAC

Create an ADHD-Friendly Personal Owner's Manual

TABLE OF CONTENTS

Patty Blinderman, PCAC, PCC

Notes

Why Create an Owner's Manual for ADHD?

Most people grow up assuming they should intuitively know how to manage daily life—schedules, tasks, relationships. But if you have ADHD, you've likely discovered that many traditional strategies don't work for your brain. That's because methods designed for neurotypical brains often lead to frustration and overwhelm for those with ADHD.

This is where the concept of a Personal Owner's Manual (POM) comes in. It's designed to be a guidebook, specifically created with your ADHD brain in mind. If you've ever felt like you needed a manual to help navigate your life, the POM is just that—an empowering tool that embraces your strengths and supports your challenges.

The Structure of the POM

The POM is organized into seven key chapters, each focusing on different areas essential to managing life with ADHD. The structure is designed to guide you through understanding yourself better and developing personalized strategies that work for your brain:

1. *Introduction to the POM and Successes*
   This chapter explains what a POM is and why it's important to build one for ADHD. It also highlights the power of focusing on successes and introduces the ADHD-Friendly Success Journal, which helps you capture your achievements, reinforce positive self-talk, and push back against negative patterns.
2. *Strengths Inventory*
   Here, you'll explore your personal strengths and learn how to leverage them in daily life. By focusing on what you're naturally good at, you can create systems that work for you rather than against you.
3. *Executive Functions*
   This chapter breaks down executive function skills, helping you identify both your strengths and areas where you may need support. Understanding executive functions is key to managing ADHD-related challenges like planning, organization, and task management.
4. *Time Management and Planning/Prioritizing Tools*
   Time management can be a significant struggle for people with ADHD. This chapter introduces ADHD-friendly tools that help you manage time effectively, emphasizing visual, concrete, and physical systems that align with how your brain processes time. There are tools that simplify planning and prioritizing tasks to help you break down complex projects into manageable steps, allowing you to stay focused and organized.
5. *Task Initiation and Dr. Dodson's ICNUP Model*
   Many people with ADHD struggle with getting started on tasks. This chapter introduces practical methods to overcome procrastination and task paralysis, including Dr. William Dodson's ICNUP model, which focuses on identifying tasks that are interesting, novel, urgent, or have personal meaning.

6. *Your ADHD-Friendly Toolbox*
   This chapter is all about building a personalized toolbox that includes all the strategies, systems, and tools that work best for you. By customizing your approaches to fit your unique needs, your POM becomes a flexible, evolving resource.
7. *Know Thyself and Customizing Your Systems*
   The final chapter is all about you—your unique needs, systems, and tools. It emphasizes that there is no "right" way to manage ADHD; there's only what works for you. By tracking your progress, noticing what helps and what doesn't, and adjusting as needed, you'll create systems that support your success over time.

Tools for Exploration

Each chapter contains specific tools designed to target challenges common with ADHD.

- Tool Defined: What the tool is for and why it's important.
- Origin Story: How and why the tool was developed, often with inspiration from ADHD research and best practices.
- How I Use It: Some tools include this section, which shares personal details on how I use the tool to support myself.
- Example: A real-life scenario or use case that illustrates how the tool works.
- Make It Yours: Customization tips and suggestions for adjusting the tool to fit your specific needs and preferences.

Flexibility and Evolution

While your needs, strengths, and challenges may change over time, your POM is designed to grow evolve with you. Each chapter provides an overall summary of its focus area and introduces the tools that will help you explore and address that area in a way that makes sense for your brain.

The POM isn't a single tool but rather a collection of resources that you can draw from as needed. It includes strategies for time management, prioritization, task initiation, emotional regulation, and more. Each tool is designed to help you address common ADHD challenges in a personalized way.

Creating your Personal Owner's Manual isn't about aiming for perfection—it's about building something that reflects your life, your strengths, and your challenges. The POM is there to support you as you navigate life with ADHD, offering practical, adaptable tools to help you struggle less and thrive more. Let's get started!

1

What a POM is and Capturing Successes

Tools:

Success Journal

Chapter 1

Introduction to the Personal Owner's Manual and the Importance of Capturing Successes

Before diving into specific tools, it's important to understand what a Personal Owner's Manual (POM) is and why it's essential for individuals with ADHD. Think of it as your ADHD-friendly guidebook, custom-made for your brain. The POM offers a flexible structure, not rigid rules, to support your unique needs and challenges.

Dr. William Dodson introduced the idea that many people with ADHD are given the wrong "manual"—full of strategies designed for neurotypical brains that don't work for us. This realization inspired the POM, which focuses on ADHD-friendly strategies tailored to your strengths and challenges. Instead of trying to fit into neurotypical systems, the POM helps you create a guide that works for you.

Why Create a Personal Owner's Manual?

Many people with ADHD struggle to fit into systems that don't account for the unique challenges ADHD brings, such as difficulties with executive function, including time management, task initiation, and emotional regulation. The POM helps address these challenges by focusing on what works best for your ADHD brain. It's a living document that evolves with you, allowing you to continuously adjust and refine your strategies over time.

Capturing Successes: Why It Matters

One of the key elements of the POM is focusing on your successes. ADHD often leads to a pattern of negative self-talk, with many people fixating on past mistakes. Capturing your successes breaks that cycle by shifting your focus to what *is working*.

The ADHD-Friendly Success Journal is introduced in this chapter to help you build a habit of recording your wins, no matter how small. Research shows that regularly acknowledging your achievements improves self-esteem, reduces anxiety, and increases motivation. By keeping track of your successes, you create a positive reinforcement loop, helping you push back against negative thoughts and build resilience.

How to Start Your POM

Starting your POM can feel overwhelming, but it doesn't need to be. Here are a few tips to get you started:
- Start small: Jot down a few things you know about yourself—what motivates you, what distracts you, and what tools help.
- Focus on progress over perfection: Your POM will evolve as you learn more about yourself. The goal is to make progress, even if it feels incomplete.

- Use what works: If you've found tools or strategies that help, include them. Your POM is about building a manual focused on what works for *your* brain.

Self-Reflection

Self-reflection is a key part of creating your POM. It helps you understand your strengths and challenges, allowing you to tailor your manual more effectively. As you work on your POM, reflect on these key areas:

- Strengths: What comes naturally to you? Where do you excel?
- Challenges: Where do you struggle the most? This will highlight which tools you need.
- Motivation: What keeps you engaged and focused?
- Energy drains: What saps your focus and energy, and how can you mitigate it?

Dr. William Dodson's Influence

Dr. Dodson's insight that many people with ADHD are given the wrong manual inspired the creation of the POM. His idea was simple: instead of trying to fit into systems designed for neurotypical brains, build a manual tailored to the way your brain works. This is the *manual* that gives you the template to bridge the gap between the idea of a POM to having a manual full of ADHD-friendly strategies that suit *your* unique needs.

Conclusion

The Personal Owner's Manual is a revolutionary approach to managing life with ADHD. It recognizes that traditional methods often fail people with ADHD, and instead offers a custom-built guide that works for you. By embracing your strengths, capturing your successes, and creating flexible systems, the POM helps you navigate life in a way that's sustainable and empowering.

Remember, the POM isn't about following rigid rules—it's about building something that evolves with you. Whether you're just starting out or refining your existing strategies, your POM will become a valuable resource for understanding and supporting your ADHD brain.

This chapter sets the stage for the rest of the book, by focusing on successes first.

Notes

Patty Blinderman, PCAC, PCC

ADHD-Friendly Success Journal

Tool Defined:

It is essential to capture successes. The ADHD-Friendly Success Journal is a tool designed for that purpose. The tool is set up to support you in writing down 3 of your successes each day. The successes can be big wins or small victories. Success can be anything that feels like a win throughout your day.

Origin Story:

I created this tool for myself a number of years ago after I first tried the "3 Successes Exercise." The exercise is based on a study done by Dr. Martin Seligman which showed that participants who wrote down three successes per day for 2 weeks had the following benefits:
- 92% reported feeling happier within 15 days
- Participants found that the results lasted at least six months
- Many participants chose to continue the exercise even after the 2 weeks ended

I liked the idea of making it easy for my brain to keep up with this by having one page with the 7 days of the week, with the numbers 1, 2, 3 for each day, so I could easily see my wins and my progress.

About the Example:

The filled-in example shows various successes, from making the bed to writing down the three successes themselves. No success is too small. We often dismiss wins as not being "big enough" to acknowledge. I have pleasantly discovered it is often the pattern of small successes that ends up having the biggest impact over time.

Make it *YOURS*:

The first step to starting your success journal is to identify when you will write down your 3 daily successes. I write my three daily successes right before I go to bed at night. After I finish, I write the next days date and add a #1 to the next line. This pulls me into writing in it again the next night. When I wake up each morning I move my success journal from my nightstand to my pillow. Because I have to move it to get into bed at night, it serves as a visual prompt to remind me to write in it.

What prompt(s) will you need to remember to do it each day?

ADHD-Friendly Success Journal

Week of: _January 15_ **to** _January 21, 2024_

Monday:
1. 1st POM Group - on time!
2. Made bed
3. Wrote 3 successes!

Tuesday:
1. Walked dogs before coffee
2. Made bed again
3. Wrote 3 successes x2!

Wednesday:
1. At work on time
2. Got milk on way home
3. Wrote 3 successes x3

Thursday:
1. Up without snoozing!
2. Cleaned up after dinner.
3. Wrote 3 successes x4!

Friday:
1. Scheduled dr. Appt!
2. Called internet company
3. Wrote 3 successes x5

Saturday:
1. Slept in without guilt!
2. Called my dad (finally!)
3. Wrote 3 successes x6!

Sunday:
1. Caught up on yard work
2. Started and finished laundry
3. Wrote 3 successes x7! Go me!

Notes:

I am loving this. It takes only 1.5-2 minutes a day. Keep going! :-)

Patty Blinderman, PCAC, PCC

ADHD-Friendly Success Journal

Week of: _____ **to** _____

Monday:	Tuesday:
1.	1.
2.	2.
3.	3.

Wednesday:	Thursday:
1.	1.
2.	2.
3.	3.

Friday:	Saturday:
1.	1.
2.	2.
3.	3.

Sunday:	Notes:
1.	
2.	
3.	

Notes

2

Strengths

Chapter 2

Focusing on Strengths

Many of us with ADHD are highly attuned to our failures. It's often easier to pinpoint where we've struggled rather than to see where we've succeeded. This focus on shortcomings can be draining, eroding self-confidence, and fueling negative self-talk. Constantly noticing what hasn't worked creates a cycle of discouragement, and in the world of ADHD, this pattern is all too common. But what if we shifted that focus? What if instead of searching for flaws, we actively sought out evidence of our strengths and successes?

In chapter 1 we began the foundation of your POM by focusing on successes. In Chapter 2 we build on successes by recognizing and amplifying your strengths. This chapter is about taking a step back from the negative lens and learning to appreciate what's working. In doing so, you'll lay the foundation for building momentum and confidence in your ability to thrive with ADHD.

Shifting from Failures to Strengths

It's a well-known fact that individuals with ADHD often struggle with executive functions, such as time management, organization, and task initiation. These areas of difficulty can make it easy to focus on where we fall short. From missed deadlines to forgotten appointments, it feels like there's always evidence of our struggles right in front of us. However, what we often overlook is that we also have strengths—sometimes hidden, sometimes right under our noses—that can help us succeed. But we have to be intentional about looking for them.

Focusing on strengths isn't just about thinking positively or glossing over real challenges. It's about understanding the unique qualities you have and finding ways to use them to your advantage. When you start your Personal Owner's Manual (POM) by acknowledging successes, you're setting yourself up for a shift in mindset. Instead of being mired in what's not working, you begin to notice what is working—and that shift is incredibly powerful.

The Power of Momentum

One of the key reasons we start the POM with a focus on successes is to build momentum. ADHD brains are wired for interest and stimulation, and successes provide that spark. Successes, even small ones, give us a sense of achievement and the motivation to keep going. The more successes you capture, the more opportunities you have to acknowledge your strengths. When you have evidence of your strengths, you create momentum you can use to tackle the areas where you struggle.

Think about it like this: when you're constantly focusing on failures, it's like trying to push a boulder uphill. It's exhausting, and eventually, you'll give up. But when you focus on strengths, it's like giving that boulder a push downhill. You gain speed, and suddenly, tasks that once felt insurmountable feel more doable. Success builds on success, creating an upward spiral, and this positive momentum is essential with ADHD.

Recognizing Patterns

Another benefit of focusing on your strengths is the ability to recognize patterns. When you look for what's going well, you begin to notice patterns in your behavior. Maybe you're great at creative problem-solving, but only when you're in a calm environment. Or perhaps you're at your best when working in short bursts rather than long stretches. Identifying these patterns is key because they provide you with a roadmap for replicating your successes in the future and for advocating for what you need to be successful.

For example, if you realize that you work most efficiently in the morning, you can structure your day to take advantage of that peak time. If you find that physical movement helps you focus, you can build short exercise breaks into your routine. Recognizing patterns allows you to make intentional choices that align with your strengths, rather than fighting against your natural tendencies.

Types of Strengths

In this chapter, we delve into various types of strengths, helping you create an inventory of the areas where you naturally excel. By understanding the different kinds of strengths, you'll have a fuller picture of what you bring to the table. Below are some of the types of strengths you'll explore in this chapter:

- **Performance Strengths:** These are the skills you demonstrate when you're performing tasks or meeting goals. It could be your ability to think outside the box, work well under pressure, or lead a team. Performance strengths can also include being detail-oriented, resourceful, or being able to see a task through from start to completion.
- **Character Strengths:** These are the qualities that define who you are. It could be your resilience in the face of adversity, your empathy for others, or your enthusiasm for learning new things. Character strengths are often the backbone of personal success, helping you push through challenges and stay motivated. For example, if you have a strong sense of curiosity, you may find it easier to dive into new projects, even if you struggle with task initiation.
- **Talents:** Talents are the innate abilities you have that come naturally. Maybe you're musically gifted, a natural artist, or you have an uncanny ability to connect with people. These talents often serve as a source of joy and fulfillment, but they can also be leveraged to create structures in your life that support your ADHD challenges. For instance, a natural storyteller might find ways to incorporate that talent into their career, or a visually creative person might use visual tools like mind maps to organize their thoughts.
- **Processing Modalities:** ADHD brains can be an advantage when harnessed effectively. Some people with ADHD are visual learners, others are auditory learners, and some learn best through movement (kinesthetic). By identifying how you process information, you can set up environments that play to your strengths. For example, if you're a visual learner, using color-coded systems, mind maps, or even visual timers might help you stay organized and on track.

Capturing Evidence of Strengths

Once you've identified your strengths, it's important to capture evidence of them. This is where keeping a success journal or log becomes invaluable. Writing down your successes, no matter how small, serves as a tangible reminder of what's working. It also gives you something to refer back to when you're feeling discouraged or overwhelmed.

Capturing evidence isn't just about boosting your confidence—it's about creating a record that you can replicate in the future. When you have a documented history of what's worked for you, you can return to those strategies when faced with similar challenges. For example, if you notice that breaking tasks into smaller chunks helped you complete a big project, you can apply that same approach to future tasks.

Here's a practical example: let's say you had a successful week where you managed to stay on top of deadlines by using a new app to set reminders. By capturing that success, you not only reinforce the positive behavior but also create a blueprint for future projects. You've identified that the combination of the app and regular check-ins worked for you, and now you can intentionally tap into that approach.

Overcoming Negative Self-Talk

One of the biggest obstacles to recognizing strengths is the pervasive negative self-talk that often accompanies ADHD. Statements like "I'm always late," "I can't focus," or "I never finish what I start" are not just unhelpful—they're also untrue. While it's easy to fall into the trap of believing these negative narratives, focusing on strengths allows you to rewrite your story.

By actively seeking out successes and strengths, you begin to quiet that inner critic. When you have concrete evidence of what's working, it becomes harder to believe the negative stories you tell yourself. Over time, this shift in focus helps to reduce feelings of shame and inadequacy, replacing them with a sense of capability and self-assurance.

Practical Tools

In this chapter, you'll find tools to help you identify and document your strengths. These tools include:

1. **Strengths Inventory:** A tool for identifying your strengths in performance, character, talents, and processing modalities. This inventory helps you see your strengths in a comprehensive way, giving you a clearer sense of where you excel.
2. **Evidence of Strengths:** A worksheet designed to help you identify patterns in your strengths that lead to successes. By recognizing what worked well in the past, you'll be better equipped to replicate those successes in the future.

Conclusion

In Chapter 2 we focus on the strengths that creats successes, allowing you to build momentum, recognize patterns, and gain a deeper understanding of how you operate best. This chapter sets the foundation for the rest of your Personal Owner's Manual, empowering you to harness your unique strengths and apply them to all areas of your life. Whether it's through a strengths inventory, a success journal, or simply acknowledging what's going well, this chapter will help you flip the script to struggling less and thriving more.

Strengths Inventory

Tool Defined:

I use this "One-Pager" tool to consolidate a list of my strengths all in one place. The strength areas included are:
- Character Strengths
- Executive Function Skills
- Performance and Talents
- Processing Modalities

To explore your strengths in these categories:
- Character Strengths: Take the free Character Strengths Survey at viacharacter.org.
- Executive Function Skills: The Executive Function Skills Questionnaire for parents or teens is available at ADDitude Magazine.
- Adult EF Skills: Dawson and Guare's questionnaire for adults can be found in their book Smart But Scattered Guide to Success by Peg Dawson and Richard Guare.
- Performance and Talents: Include athletic, musical, or other talents here.
- Processing modalities: Which ways do you learn best? Check ones that apply to you.

Origin Story:

The Strengths Inventory is a Working Memory tool I created to help me remember my strengths more easily. After taking the free VIA Character Strengths survey offered at viacharacter.org, I wanted a simple way to keep my top strengths visible. The survey results list 24 character strengths in order from strongest to weakest, and the Strengths Inventory includes space to list your top 8 strengths.

Using Dawson and Guare's Executive Functions Skills Questionnaire, I identify my 3 strongest and 3 weakest EF skills and list them on this form. (See the "Tool Defined" section above for where to find the questionnaire.)

About the Example:

This example is based on a previous coaching client (name changed). Note the "Other Strengths" at the bottom. What other strengths would you add to your inventory?

Make it *YOURS*:

Are you a visual processor? How can you capture your strengths visually? What layout works best for you? These tools are provided as examples. If my tool doesn't suit your needs, adapt the concept to create something that works better for you.

Strengths Inventory

Name: Sarah T.

Date: January 8, 2024

Character Strengths:

1. Honesty
2. Love of Learning
3. Bravery
4. Kindness
5. Perspective
6. Judgment
7. Humor
8. Love

Executive Function Strengths

1. Metacognition
2. Time Management
3. Organization

Executive Function Challenges

1. Working Memory
2. Flexibility
3. Emotional Control

Performance Strengths/Talents

1. Computer programming/technology
2. Running
3. Playing piano
4.

Processing Modalities

When learning something new, you need to use...

- ☑ Auditory (hear information)
- ☐ Conceptual (understand the big picture)
- ☐ Kinesthetic (move around)
- ☑ Visual (see information)
- ☑ Verbal (talk through thoughts)
- ☑ Tactile (touch or feel)
- ☐ Emotional (have a positive emotion)
- ☐ Intuitive (sense to understand)

Other Strengths/Notes

Able to ask for help when needed, even when uncomfortable.

Positive energy

Good at making friends

Patty Blinderman, PCAC, PCC

Strengths Inventory

Name:_____   Date:_____

Character Strengths:

1._____   5._____
2._____   6._____
3._____   7._____
4._____   8._____

Executive Function Strengths   ## Executive Function Challenges

1._____   1._____
2._____   2._____
3._____   3._____

Performance Strengths/Talents

1._____
2._____
3._____
4._____

Processing Modalities

When learning something new, you need to use...

❑ Auditory (hear information)   ❑ Verbal (talk through thoughts)
❑ Conceptual (understand the big picture)   ❑ Tactile (touch or feel)
❑ Kinesthetic (move around)   ❑ Emotional (have a positive emotion)
❑ Visual (see information)   ❑ Intuitive (sense to understand)

Other Strengths/Notes

_____
_____
_____

Notes

Evidence of Strengths

Tool Defined:

This tool helps you capture specific evidence of your strengths. A list of strengths alone is just a list of words. Without evidence, it's hard to see how these strengths manifest in your life. This tool is designed to provide a way to identify and document how your strengths show up in real situations.

Origin Story:

I created this tool to better understand and utilize my strengths after taking the VIA Character Strengths Survey and identifying my top strengths. Initially, I was unsure how to apply strengths like "Love of Learning" and "Appreciation of Beauty and Excellence" to improve my life. By examining successes through the lens of these strengths, I developed this tool to record my insights. Over time, I noticed patterns and began using these strengths intentionally to tackle challenges outside my comfort zone.

Now, I review my successes each month and use this tool to gather more evidence of my strengths. Having concrete examples has made this tool incredibly valuable and empowering.

About the Example:

"Mike" (name changed), a client of mine, agreed to allow me to share his example. Some successes appeared in multiple strength areas (e.g.., "Joined a book club" under both "Love of Learning" and "Bravery"). When Mike felt uncomfortable stepping outside his comfort zone, he looked at his examples of bravery, which provided evidence that he could do it, making it easier for him to use his bravery in new situations.

Make it *YOURS*:

Remember, a list of strengths without specific evidence is just a list of words. What category or specific strength would be the easiest place for you to begin collecting evidence? If the mind-map layout of this tool doesn't inspire you to use it, what changes can you make so it works better for you?

Evidence of Strengths

EF Strengths

Planning

- Family calendar on wall in kitchen.
- Planned surprise anniversary trip
- Created a "savings thermometer" for family vacation (it got everyone focused on the goal!)

Working Memory

- Visual tools (post-its)
- Checklist for groceries
- Captured the process for monthly budgeting so I can follow it each month.

Flexibility

- Willing to try systems out
- Creating work-from-home areas so I can move to an alternate work area when I'm bored with the first one.
- Let family members know I need time to adjust to new plans and ideas

Love of Learning

- Social Media webinar
- Joined book club

"Mike's" Evidence of Strengths

Processing Modalities

Visual

- Sketches on post-its
- Family calendar on wall in kitchen
- Planner open on desk
- Analog clock in office

VIA Strengths

Kindness

- Offered to help with planning dinner
- Outsourced yard work (company needed work & I didn't want to do it! Kind to them AND me!)

Bravery

- Joined book club
- Asked for help with taxes
- Joined new gym
- Advocated for myself around how change takes time for me to adjust to (and can make me irritable).

Humor

- Sketches on post-its
- Fun pictures of kids on phone lock screen
- Fun mantras like, "Whoever has the most fun wins" to get out of perfectionism.

Evidence of Strengths

Evidence
of
Strengths

Patty Blinderman, PCAC, PCC

Patty Blinderman, PCAC, PCC

3

Executive Function Skills

Tools:

Executive Function Skills Tool

Understanding Executive Function Skills

Chapter 3 dives into one of the most critical aspects of ADHD management: executive function (EF) skills. These are the mental processes that allow us to plan, focus, remember instructions, and start and finish tasks. However, for those of us with ADHD, EF skills can often be weak or inconsistent, leading to frustration and difficulty in managing daily life. Understanding how these skills work, and more importantly, how ADHD impacts them, is essential for creating strategies that make sense for your brain.

What Are Executive Function Skills?

Executive function skills are often referred to as the "control center" of the brain, guiding and organizing our behavior. Dr. Thomas Brown, a leading ADHD researcher, likens executive functions to a conductor in an orchestra, ensuring that all the different instruments (our thoughts, actions, and behaviors) are in sync. Without a conductor, the orchestra would fall into chaos, much like how our daily lives can feel when executive function skills aren't working well.

These skills are crucial for:
- **Planning and organizing** tasks.
- **Inhibiting** impulses or distractions.
- **Shifting** focus from one task to another.
- **Managing time** effectively.
- **Remembering details** and instructions.

For individuals with ADHD, these processes can be disrupted. What might seem like a simple task to others—such as planning your day—can require enormous effort and often leads to overwhelm or avoidance.

The 12 Executive Function Skills

As outlined by Dawson and Guare in their *Smart but Scattered* series, executive function skills can be broken down into 12 key areas. Each of these skills plays a unique role in helping you manage tasks and life efficiently, and understanding how ADHD affects them is crucial.

1. **Response Inhibition**
   The ability to think before acting. For those with ADHD, impulsivity can lead to acting before thinking, which might result in forgotten tasks or rash decisions.
2. **Working Memory**
   This is your brain's ability to hold onto information while you work with it. If you've ever forgotten why you walked into a room, you've experienced a lapse in working memory. ADHD can make retaining and manipulating information a major challenge.

3. **Emotional Control**
Managing emotions appropriately is another function of executive skills. ADHD can make emotional regulation difficult, leading to heightened responses to stress or frustration.

4. **Task Initiation**
Starting a task is often one of the hardest things for individuals with ADHD. It's not that we don't want to do something—it's that getting the momentum to begin can feel like an insurmountable obstacle.

5. **Sustained Attention**
Staying focused, especially on tasks that are boring or difficult, can be particularly challenging. ADHD makes it hard to maintain attention for extended periods, leading to unfinished projects.

6. **Planning/Prioritization**
Planning and deciding what needs to be done first is a core executive function skill. With ADHD, it can be tough to break down large tasks into manageable steps, which leads to overwhelm.

7. **Organization**
Keeping track of physical and mental materials is another key EF skill. Disorganization, whether it's cluttered spaces or chaotic thoughts, is a common challenge for people with ADHD.

8. **Time Management**
Time blindness—the inability to accurately gauge how long tasks will take or how much time is available—is a well-known struggle for those with ADHD. This impacts everything from getting places on time to meeting deadlines.

9. **Goal-Directed Persistence**
Sticking with a task until it's completed, especially long-term goals, can feel nearly impossible with ADHD. We often lose interest or move onto something else before finishing.

10. **Flexibility**
The ability to adapt and shift focus when circumstances change is another executive function skill. People with ADHD may struggle when plans suddenly change or when they're required to shift gears quickly.

11. **Metacognition**
This is the ability to step back and assess how you're doing with a task—essentially thinking about your own thinking. ADHD often makes it difficult to recognize when something isn't working and adjust accordingly.

12. **Stress Tolerance**
Managing stress in healthy ways is a vital executive function. ADHD can cause everyday challenges to feel overwhelming, making it harder to stay calm and focused under pressure.

How ADHD Impacts Executive Function

For most people, these executive function skills work automatically in the background, helping them navigate life with relative ease. However, with ADHD, the "conductor" isn't always as effective. This can lead to:
- **Impulsivity:** Difficulty pausing to think through actions.
- **Forgetfulness:** Inability to retain important information in the moment.

- **Disorganization:** Struggles with keeping both physical spaces and thoughts in order.
- **Difficulty managing emotions:** Overreacting to stress, frustration, or disappointment.
- **Time struggles:** Chronically underestimating how long tasks will take, leading to missed deadlines and frustration.

Thomas Brown's View on Executive Function

Thomas Brown describes executive functions as the brain's conductor because they help to synchronize all of our mental processes. When the conductor is off, so is the entire performance. Brown's analogy is helpful in understanding why ADHD impacts daily life so deeply. It's not about lacking intelligence or motivation—it's that the systems that guide us through tasks and life are not operating as efficiently as they could be.

Recognizing Strengths in Executive Function

While the impact of ADHD on executive function skills can be frustrating, it's important to remember that there are strengths that accompany ADHD as well. Many people with ADHD excel in creativity, problem-solving, and thinking outside the box. By understanding where your executive function skills may need support, you can create systems that play to your strengths and compensate for weaker areas.

For example, if you struggle with working memory, you might develop a habit of writing things down immediately. If time management is a challenge, setting alarms and using external timers can help keep you on track.

Using the POM to Address Executive Function Challenges

In this chapter, the Executive Function Skills tool is designed to help you identify your unique executive function strengths and weaknesses. Whether it's creating a plan for task initiation or developing a system to stay organized, the goal is to find ADHD-friendly strategies that help manage the daily impacts of executive function challenges.

The *Smart but Scattered* books offer a wealth of strategies for each of the 12 executive function areas. By incorporating their insights into your Personal Owner's Manual, you can create a plan that not only acknowledges where you need support but also celebrates where you thrive.

Conclusion

Understanding executive function skills is key to building a life that works with your ADHD, rather than against it. By identifying where you excel and where you need support, you can create systems that help you manage day-to-day challenges more effectively. In Chapter 3, you'll explore your executive function skills, growing your awareness of which are your three stronger and weaker skills. In Chapter 4 you'll do a deeper dive into the EF skills of Time Management and Planning and Prioritizing and Chapter 5 focuses on the EF skill of Task Initiation.

Executive Function Skills

Tool Defined:

The Executive Function Skills Survey helps you identify and understand your strengths and weaknesses in various executive function skills. These skills include areas like planning, organization, time management, and self-regulation. By pinpointing where you excel and where you may need support, you can develop strategies to enhance your daily functioning and overall productivity.

To explore more information on executive function skills:
- **Teens and Parents:** The Executive Function Skills Questionnaire can be found at ADDitude Magazine.
- **Adults:** Dawson and Guare's Executive Functions Skills Questionnaire is available in their book Smart But Scattered Guide to Success by Peg Dawson and Richard Guare.

Origin Story:

I created the Executive Function Skills Survey to use in my Personal Owner's Manual (POM) groups and courses to support participants to pinpoint their 3 strongest and 3 weakest executive function skills and have the description of each on the same page. By using a simple "+" and "-" rating system, it is easy to identify strengths and weaknesses at a glance.

About the Example:

As this is a survey to use during my POM groups and courses, a simple example showing what it might look like after it is completed is provided. Some of the skills can show up as a strength in one area and weakness in another. To reflect this, these skills are marked as +/-.

Make it *YOURS*:

Understanding your executive function skills can greatly enhance your ability to manage everyday tasks. What are your strongest executive function skills? Where do you need more support? The goal is to gain a clear picture of your executive function profile and use this knowledge to set yourself up to shift from struggling to thriving with ADHD.

Executive Function Skills

Based on Dawson & Guare's work in *Smart But Scattered Guide to Success*

EF Skill	Description	Self-Evaluation (+ or −)
Metacognition	The ability to take a birds-eye view of yourself in a situation and evaluate how you are doing. (Thinking about your thinking.)	+
Working Memory	The ability to hold information in memory while performing complex tasks.	+/−
Emotional Control	The ability to manage emotions in order to complete tasks, achieve goals, or control and direct behavior.	+
Response Inhibition	The capacity to think before you act or say something.	−
Sustained Attention	The ability to maintain focus on a task despite distractions or boredom.	+/−
Task Initiation	The ability to start tasks or projects without procrastination.	−
Planning/Prioritizing	The ability to connect present thinking to future outcomes. To be able to create a roadmap to reach a goal or complete a project.	+/−
Organization	The ability to create and maintain systems for physical things as well as the ability to structure thoughts into spoken and written language.	+
Time Management	The capacity to have internal awareness of the passage of time. To estimate how much time you have, and use it to stay within time limits and meet deadlines.	−
Goal-Directed Persistence	The ability to finish what you start without being distracted by competing interests.	+/−
Flexibility	The ability to change plans due to obstacles, setbacks, new information, or mistakes.	+/−
Stress Tolerance	The ability to cope with uncertainty and thrive in stressful situations.	+/−

Strengths	Weaknesses
Metacognition	Response Inhibition
Emotional Control	Task Initiation
Organization	Time Management

Executive Function Skills

Based on Dawson & Guare's work in *Smart But Scattered Guide to Success*

EF Skill	Description	Self-Evaluation (+ or −)
Metacognition	The ability to take a birds-eye view of yourself in a situation and evaluate how you are doing. (Thinking about your thinking.)	
Working Memory	The ability to hold information in memory while performing complex tasks.	
Emotional Control	The ability to manage emotions in order to complete tasks, achieve goals, or control and direct behavior.	
Response Inhibition	The capacity to think before you act or say something.	
Sustained Attention	The ability to maintain focus on a task despite distractions or boredom.	
Task Initiation	The ability to start tasks or projects without procrastination.	
Planning/Prioritizing	The ability to connect present thinking to future outcomes. To be able to create a roadmap to reach a goal or complete a project.	
Organization	The ability to create and maintain systems for physical things as well as the ability to structure thoughts into spoken and written language.	
Time Management	The capacity to have internal awareness of the passage of time. To estimate how much time you have, and use it to stay within time limits and meet deadlines.	
Goal-Directed Persistence	The ability to finish what you start without being distracted by competing interests.	
Flexibility	The ability to change plans due to obstacles, setbacks, new information, or mistakes.	
Stress Tolerance	The ability to cope with uncertainty and thrive in stressful situations.	

Strengths	Weaknesses

 Patty Blinderman, PCAC, PCC

Notes

Patty Blinderman, PCAC, PCC

4

Time Management and Planning/Prioritizing

Tools:

Monthly Calendar
Monthly Planner
Weekly Calendar (Sun-Sat)
Weekly Calendar (Mon-Sun)

Weekly Planner
Daily Planner
Stovetop Prioritizer
Bracket Your Priorities

Time Management, Planning, and Prioritizing

In Chapter 4, we take a closer look at two executive function (EF) skills that often present significant challenges for those of us with ADHD: **time management** and **planning and prioritizing**. These skills are essential for navigating the demands of daily life, yet they are also the areas where ADHD tends to cause the most disruption. This chapter is designed to not only highlight how ADHD impacts these skills but also provide practical, ADHD-friendly tools to help you improve in these areas.

Why Time Management, Planning, and Prioritizing Are So Important

Time management and the ability to plan and prioritize are central to managing daily tasks, meeting deadlines, and achieving long-term goals. When these skills aren't functioning optimally, it can lead to feelings of overwhelm, missed deadlines, procrastination, and a constant sense of playing catch-up. For individuals with ADHD, the challenges can feel even more pronounced due to something known as "time blindness," where the perception of time is skewed, making it difficult to accurately gauge how long tasks will take or how much time is available.

Time Management and ADHD

Time management is the skill of organizing your time effectively so that tasks are completed efficiently. For individuals with ADHD, time can often feel abstract. The ability to recognize how long something will take, to estimate how much time is needed for a task, or even to remember time-sensitive commitments can be impacted. ADHD tends to create a phenomenon where time feels like it's either "now" or "not now," which makes planning ahead and sticking to schedules particularly difficult.

Common Time Management Challenges in ADHD:

Starting your POM can feel overwhelming, but it doesn't need to be. Here are a few tips to get you started:

- **Time blindness:** The inability to sense time accurately.
- **Procrastination:** Difficulty starting tasks or delaying them until the last minute.
- **Underestimating how long tasks will take:** This leads to incomplete tasks or missed deadlines.
- **Inconsistent focus:** Difficulty staying on track when there's no immediate urgency.

Planning and Prioritizing with ADHD

Planning and prioritizing involve deciding what needs to be done, in what order, and how to allocate your time effectively. For people with ADHD, this process can feel overwhelming. Breaking down large tasks into smaller, manageable steps, identifying what is most important, and sticking to a plan can be particularly challenging. Without strong prioritization skills, we can end up focusing on tasks that feel urgent but may not actually be important, leaving truly critical tasks unfinished.

ADHD Challenges with Planning and Prioritizing:

- **Difficulty breaking down large tasks:** Projects can feel so overwhelming that starting them feels impossible.
- **Struggles with prioritization:** Everything can feel equally important, so choosing what's most important is a challenge. This often leads to doing easy tasks first or tackling tasks that are less essential.
- **Difficulty following through:** Even if a plan is made, sticking to it consistently can be a struggle.

Tools to Support Time Management, Planning, and Prioritizing

While these challenges are very real, the good news is that there are strategies and tools that can help you work with your brain, not against it. This chapter offers a variety of tools to support better time management and prioritization, designed specifically with ADHD in mind.

1. Monthly, Weekly, and Daily Planners

These visual, external, and concrete tools help you break down your time and tasks into more manageable chunks. By using monthly, weekly, and daily planners, you can get a clearer picture of upcoming commitments and deadlines. These planners allow you to create structure and routine, making it easier to see what's coming up and lessen last-minute scrambles.

- **Monthly Planners:** Great for getting a bird's-eye view of the month ahead, including major deadlines, appointments, and goals.
- **Weekly Planners:** A more detailed breakdown of what's coming up each week, allowing you to see when smaller tasks or appointments are scheduled.
- **Daily Planners:** Focus on the tasks that need to be done each day. This planner helps ensure that you're taking action on your priorities and prevents tasks from slipping through the cracks.

These tools provide structure and reduce the need to constantly keep everything in your head, which can be exhausting. By externalizing these tasks, you can better manage your time and energy.

2. Stovetop Prioritization Tool

This tool helps you visualize and manage your priorities using the analogy of a stovetop with different burners. Imagine you have four burners on your stovetop—each burner represents a different area of your life (e.g., work, family, self-care, and personal projects). The idea is to recognize that only a few things can be "on the front burner" at once, meaning that you can't focus on everything all at the same time.

The stovetop prioritization tool encourages you to:

- **Identify what's on your front burner:** These are the tasks or goals that need your immediate attention.
- **Move less urgent tasks to the back burner:** These are tasks that are important but can wait until you have more time or energy.
- **Recognize when a burner is too full:** If too many tasks are vying for attention, something might boil over. This tool encourages you to focus only on a few priorities at a time to avoid burnout.

This tool is especially helpful for those with ADHD who tend to overcommit or feel like they need to do everything at once.

3. Bracket Your Priorities Tool

Inspired by March Madness sports brackets, this tool helps you narrow down a long list of priorities into a more manageable set. When everything feels urgent or important, the bracket system forces you to compare tasks or goals at a time, deciding which is more critical in the moment. This head-to-head comparison helps you work through a long list of to-dos, ultimately leaving you with the top priorities that truly need your focus.

The Bracket Your Priorities Too allows you to:

- **List all your priorities:** Writing down everything that feels like it needs to be done in a day gets it out of your head and into a list.
- **Advance the winners:** As you compare and identify priorities, the most important ones move forward, similar to a tournament bracket.
- **Identify your top priorities:** Once you've worked through the entire list, you'll have a clear set of priorities to focus on.

This tool is excellent for those who struggle with feeling overwhelmed by too many tasks or for individuals who find it difficult to know where to start.

Why These Tools Work for ADHD Brains

The tools in this chapter are designed to address the unique ways in which ADHD impacts time management, planning, and prioritizing. They help to break down large, overwhelming tasks into smaller, more manageable steps and externalize the process so you don't have to rely on working memory alone.

- **Planners:** Provide a visual and structured way to track tasks and time, reducing the cognitive load of remembering everything.
- **Stovetop Prioritization Tool:** Helps manage competing priorities by acknowledging that not everything can be addressed at once.
- **Bracket Your Priorities Tool:** Simplifies the decision-making process by helping you identify what's truly important.

By using these tools, you create systems that work with your ADHD brain, helping you manage your time more effectively and focus on the tasks that matter most.

Conclusion

Time management, planning, and prioritizing are areas where ADHD can wreak havoc, but they are also skills that can be strengthened with the right strategies and tools. By incorporating tools like planners, the Stovetop Prioritization Tool, and the Bracket Your Priorities tool into your Personal Owner's Manual, you can create a roadmap for tackling your tasks, identifying your priorities, and managing your time.

Patty Blinderman, PCAC, PCC

Monthly Calendar

Tool Defined:
The Monthly Calendar is designed to help you organize and track important dates throughout the month. With a simple, timeless design, this calendar can be used month after month, year after year, making it an essential tool for managing your schedule effectively.

Origin Story:
I created the Monthly Calendar out of a need for a flexible and reusable way to keep track of key dates and events. Traditional calendars often come prefilled with holidays and dates that may not be relevant to everyone, leaving little room for personal plans. By keeping the calendar blank, I wanted to provide a tool that could be customized to fit anyone's unique schedule, no matter the month or year.

How I Use It:
I use the Monthly Calendar to stay on top of important dates such as birthdays, anniversaries, holidays, medical appointments, travel plans, and school events. At the beginning of each month, I fill in the calendar with these key dates, ensuring that I have a clear overview of what's coming up. The blank format allows me to focus solely on the events that matter most to me, without the distraction of pre-filled dates or unnecessary details. Because it's reusable, I can easily adapt it for any month, making it a reliable part of my monthly planning routine.

About the Example:
I used the Monthly Calendar to organize a particularly busy period that included a family birthday, Thanksgiving, my book club, and travel plans. By mapping out these dates on the calendar, I was able to visualize my commitments at a glance and plan accordingly. The simplicity of the blank format allowed me to prioritize what was most important and avoid overcommitting myself.

Make it *YOURS*:
The beauty of the Monthly Calendar lies in its flexibility. You can use it to track whatever dates and events are most relevant to you, whether they're personal, professional, or a mix of both. Customize it to fit your planning style by adding color codes, notes, or even stickers to make it more engaging. Since the calendar is timeless, it's an investment in your organization that you can return to month after month. Whether you prefer to plan in advance or take things one day at a time, the Monthly Calendar is a tool that adapts to your needs, helping you stay organized and on top of your schedule.

Sunday	Monday	Tuesday	Wednesday	Thursday	Friday	Saturday
			1 ☐ Plan my month	2	3	4
5	6	7	8	9	10	11
12	13 ☐ Book Club	14	15	16	17	18
19	20	21	22	23 Thanksgiving	24	25
26 Marc's Birthday	27 ☐ Plan my month	28	29	30	1	2

C O N F E R E N C E

Sunday	Monday	Tuesday	Wednesday	Thursday	Friday	Saturday

Notes

Monthly Planner

Tool Defined:

The Monthly Planner is designed to help you stay organized and focused on your goals throughout the month. It provides a clear, visual way to manage your tasks, set intentions, and track your progress, supporting you to make the most of your time and achieve more of your goals.

Origin Story:

I wanted a tool similar to my Weekly Planner to help plan my month. This not only helps me list out my tasks but also allows me to visualize the time commitment each task requires. This tool has become an essential part of my routine, helping me stay on track more easily throughout the month.

How I Use It:

At the start of each month, I use the space at the top of the planner to set a clear monthly goal. I also decide on a reward for reaching this goal, if needed. Step 1 involves listing all the tasks I need to accomplish this month in the top half of the form. There are 21 spaces for tasks, and next to each task, I color in the time circles to estimate how long each will take—one full circle for an hour, half for 30 minutes, etc. I also use the small line to the left to indicate which week I plan to tackle each task.

In Step 2, I write the tasks by week in the bottom half of the form. There are dedicated sections for weeks 1 through 4, plus an extra space for tasks I might push to next month. This section also includes 10 time circles per week, allowing me to plan up to 10 hours of tasks weekly. This visual breakdown allows me to adjust my plans, if needed, and avoid over-committing my time.

About the Example:

I chose November to highlight because it is always a busy month for me. I listed all upcoming tasks in Step 1, including work and home/family tasks such as preparing for Thanksgiving and getting the oil changed in my car. I resisted the perfectionism temptation to fill in every space. I estimated the time for each task and noted the weeks I aimed to complete them. In Step 2, I distributed these tasks across the four weeks of the month so I could see them more easily.

Make it *YOURS*:

Customize it to fit your planning style. Use it to set intentions, manage your tasks, and track your time visually.

 Patty Blinderman, PCAC, PCC

Monthly Planner

Month/Year November 2023

STEP 1 — Monthly To-Dos

Week	Time Est.	To-Do
1	●○	Monthly Planning
2	●○	AF Event Calendar
1	●○	AF Event Slides
4	●○	Confirm Client's Dec. Sched.
1-4	●●	Plan/Record Podcasts (x4)
	○○	
	○○	

Week	Time Est.	To-Do
3	●○	Bookkeeping
2	●●●	Make AF Planners
2	●●	AF Planner Course: break into steps
4	●●	Christmas Prep: Frame pics
3	●●	Buy SS Ornaments
	○○	
	○○	

Week	Time Est.	To-Do
1	●●	Schedule Oil Change
1-2	●●	Read Book Club book
3-4	●●	Thanksgiving Prep: Shopping
3-4	●●	Company (airport, etc)
4	●○	Take family pic
	○○	
	○○	

STEP 2 — Weekly To-Dos

Week 1
Available Time: ●●●●● ●●●●●

- ● Monthly Planning
- ● AF Event Slides
- ●● Schedule Oil change
- ●● Plan/Record Podcasts
- ●● Read Book Club book

Week 2
Available Time: ●●●●● ●●●●●

- ●● AF Planner Course: break into steps
- ● AF Event Calendar
- ●●● Make AF Planners
- ●● Plan/Record Podcasts
- ●● Read Book Club book

Week 3
Available Time: ●●●●● ●●●●○

- ● Bookkeeping
- ●● Buy SS Ornaments
- ●● Thanksgiving Prep: Shopping
- ●● Company (airport, etc)
- ●● Plan/Record Podcasts

Week 4
Available Time: ●●●●● ●●●●●

- ● Confirm Client's Dec. Sched.
- ●● Christmas Prep: Frame pics
- ●● Thanksgiving Prep: Shopping
- ●● Plan/Record Podcasts
- ● Take family pic

Next Month

Monthly Planner

Month/Year_____

STEP 1   Monthly To-Dos

Week	Time Est.	To-Do	Week	Time Est.	To-Do	Week	Time Est.	To-Do
⃝ ⃝	_____	⃝ ⃝	_____	⃝ ⃝	_____
⃝ ⃝	_____	⃝ ⃝	_____	⃝ ⃝	_____
⃝ ⃝	_____	⃝ ⃝	_____	⃝ ⃝	_____
⃝ ⃝	_____	⃝ ⃝	_____	⃝ ⃝	_____
⃝ ⃝	_____	⃝ ⃝	_____	⃝ ⃝	_____
⃝ ⃝	_____	⃝ ⃝	_____	⃝ ⃝	_____
⃝ ⃝	_____	⃝ ⃝	_____	⃝ ⃝	_____

STEP 2   Weekly To-Dos

Week 1	Week 2	Week 3	Week 4	Next Month
Available Time:	Available Time:	Available Time:	Available Time:	
⃝⃝⃝⃝⃝	⃝⃝⃝⃝⃝	⃝⃝⃝⃝⃝	⃝⃝⃝⃝⃝	
⃝⃝⃝⃝⃝	⃝⃝⃝⃝⃝	⃝⃝⃝⃝⃝	⃝⃝⃝⃝⃝	

Weekly Calendar
(Sunday - Saturday)

Tool Defined:

This is a blank template designed to help you see your time and commitments for a week, with slots available in 15-minute increments daily from 6 am to 5 pm. This analog tool allows you to map out your week in a concrete, external, and visual way, helping you balance your scheduled commitments with time for essential tasks and activities.

Origin Story:

I created this when I couldn't find a planner layout that included 15-minute increments that worked for me. By breaking down the day into smaller, manageable intervals, I found it easier to see the time in my week and ensure that all my priorities were accounted for. Even though I use an online calendar to keep up with my appointments, I always use this physical planner to write out my weekly schedule. Using pen and paper better supports my brain to navigate my time with more ease.

How I Use It:

I start by filling in all my scheduled appointments, such as meetings, work commitments, and social engagements. With the 15-minute increments up until 5 pm, I can be specific about when and how long these commitments will take. Once all the appointments are in place, I look for open spaces in my week. These gaps become opportunities to block out time for tasks and unscheduled priorities. I use different colors for these time blocks, making it easy to distinguish between various types of activities at a glance.

About the Example:

In a recent week I had several client meetings and a couple of personal appointments already scheduled. After filling these in, I used a yellow highlighter to show blocks of time I had available to complete unscheduled tasks. Seeing my time in this visual way helps me complete my plans with greater ease.

Make it *YOURS*:

The Weekly Time Planner is a versatile tool that you can tailor to your specific needs. Whether you have a packed week or some flexibility, this schedule allows you to see your time clearly and make informed decisions about how to use it. Experiment with different colors to categorize your activities and make the schedule visually appealing and easy to read.

Weekly Calendar

Nov. 5	Nov. 6	Nov. 7	Nov. 8	Nov. 9	Nov. 10	Nov. 11
SUNDAY	**MONDAY**	**TUESDAY**	**WEDNESDAY**	**THURSDAY**	**FRIDAY**	**SATURDAY**
6	6	6	6	6	6	6
:15	:15	:15	:15	:15	:15	:15
:30	:30	:30	:30	:30	:30	:30
:45	:45	:45	:45	:45	:45	:45
7	7	7	7	7	7 Car Service App.	7
:15	:15	:15	:15	:15	:15	:15
:30	:30	:30	:30	:30 30 min	:30	:30
:45	:45	:45	:45	:45	:45	:45
8	8	8	8	8 Client - Zoom	8	8
:15	:15 1 hr	:15	:15 1 hr	:15	:15 1 hr	:15
:30	:30	:30 2 hrs	:30	:30	:30	:30
:45	:45	:45	:45	:45	:45	:45
9	9 Client - FT	9	9 Meeting	9	9 Meeting	9
:15	:15	:15	:15	:15 1 hr	:15	:15
:30	:30	:30	:30	:30	:30	:30
:45	:45	:45	:45	:45	:45	:45
10	10	10 Client - FT	10	10 Client - Phone	10	10
:15	:15	:15	:15	:15	:15	:15
:30	:30	:30	:30	:30	:30	:30
:45	:45	:45	:45	:45	:45	:45
11	11	11	11 AF-Account Partners	11	11	11
:15	:15 3 hrs	:15 1 hr	:15	:15 1 hr	:15	:15
:30	:30	:30	:30	:30	:30	:30
:45	:45	:45	:45	:45	:45	:45
12	12	12 Client - FT	12	12 Additude Webinar	12 AF-Power Hour: POM	12
:15	:15	:15	:15 1 hr	:15	:15	:15
:30	:30	:30	:30	:30	:30	:30
:45	:45	:45	:45	:45	:45	:45
1	1	1 LUNCH	1 LUNCH	1 LUNCH	1 DONE!	1
:15	:15 LUNCH	:15	:15	:15	:15	:15
:30	:30	:30	:30	:30	:30	:30
:45	:45	:45	:45	:45	:45 LUNCH	:45
2	2 Meeting	2 Client - Zoom	2	2	2	2
:15	:15	:15	:15 1 hr	:15 1 hr	:15	:15
:30	:30	:30	:30	:30	:30	:30
:45	:45	:45	:45	:45	:45	:45
3	3	3 DONE!	3 DONE!	3 DONE!	3	3
:15	:15	:15	:15	:15	:15	:15
:30	:30	:30	:30	:30	:30	:30
:45	:45	:45	:45	:45	:45	:45
4	4	4	4	4	4	4
:15	:15 DONE!	:15	:15	:15	:15	:15
:30	:30	:30	:30	:30	:30	:30
:45	:45	:45	:45	:45	:45	:45
5	5	5	5	5	5	5
:30	:30	:30	:30	:30	:30	:30
6	6	6	6	6	6	6
:30	:30	:30	:30	:30	:30	:30
7	7	7	7	7	7	7
:30	:30	:30	:30	:30	:30	:30
8	8	8	8	8	8	8
:30	:30	:30	:30	:30	:30	:30
9	9	9	9	9	9	9

Patty Blinderman, PCAC, PCC

Weekly Calendar

SUNDAY	MONDAY	TUESDAY	WEDNESDAY	THURSDAY	FRIDAY	SATURDAY
6	6	6	6	6	6	6
:15	:15	:15	:15	:15	:15	:15
:30	:30	:30	:30	:30	:30	:30
:45	:45	:45	:45	:45	:45	:45
7	7	7	7	7	7	7
:15	:15	:15	:15	:15	:15	:15
:30	:30	:30	:30	:30	:30	:30
:45	:45	:45	:45	:45	:45	:45
8	8	8	8	8	8	8
:15	:15	:15	:15	:15	:15	:15
:30	:30	:30	:30	:30	:30	:30
:45	:45	:45	:45	:45	:45	:45
9	9	9	9	9	9	9
:15	:15	:15	:15	:15	:15	:15
:30	:30	:30	:30	:30	:30	:30
:45	:45	:45	:45	:45	:45	:45
10	10	10	10	10	10	10
:15	:15	:15	:15	:15	:15	:15
:30	:30	:30	:30	:30	:30	:30
:45	:45	:45	:45	:45	:45	:45
11	11	11	11	11	11	11
:15	:15	:15	:15	:15	:15	:15
:30	:30	:30	:30	:30	:30	:30
:45	:45	:45	:45	:45	:45	:45
12	12	12	12	12	12	12
:15	:15	:15	:15	:15	:15	:15
:30	:30	:30	:30	:30	:30	:30
:45	:45	:45	:45	:45	:45	:45
1	1	1	1	1	1	1
:15	:15	:15	:15	:15	:15	:15
:30	:30	:30	:30	:30	:30	:30
:45	:45	:45	:45	:45	:45	:45
2	2	2	2	2	2	2
:15	:15	:15	:15	:15	:15	:15
:30	:30	:30	:30	:30	:30	:30
:45	:45	:45	:45	:45	:45	:45
3	3	3	3	3	3	3
:15	:15	:15	:15	:15	:15	:15
:30	:30	:30	:30	:30	:30	:30
:45	:45	:45	:45	:45	:45	:45
4	4	4	4	4	4	4
:15	:15	:15	:15	:15	:15	:15
:30	:30	:30	:30	:30	:30	:30
:45	:45	:45	:45	:45	:45	:45
5	5	5	5	5	5	5
:30	:30	:30	:30	:30	:30	:30
6	6	6	6	6	6	6
:30	:30	:30	:30	:30	:30	:30
7	7	7	7	7	7	7
:30	:30	:30	:30	:30	:30	:30
8	8	8	8	8	8	8
:30	:30	:30	:30	:30	:30	:30
9	9	9	9	9	9	9

Patty Blinderman, PCAC, PCC

Weekly Calendar

MONDAY	TUESDAY	WEDNESDAY	THURSDAY	FRIDAY	SATURDAY	SUNDAY
6	6	6	6	6	6	6
:15	:15	:15	:15	:15	:15	:15
:30	:30	:30	:30	:30	:30	:30
:45	:45	:45	:45	:45	:45	:45
7	7	7	7	7	7	7
:15	:15	:15	:15	:15	:15	:15
:30	:30	:30	:30	:30	:30	:30
:45	:45	:45	:45	:45	:45	:45
8	8	8	8	8	8	8
:15	:15	:15	:15	:15	:15	:15
:30	:30	:30	:30	:30	:30	:30
:45	:45	:45	:45	:45	:45	:45
9	9	9	9	9	9	9
:15	:15	:15	:15	:15	:15	:15
:30	:30	:30	:30	:30	:30	:30
:45	:45	:45	:45	:45	:45	:45
10	10	10	10	10	10	10
:15	:15	:15	:15	:15	:15	:15
:30	:30	:30	:30	:30	:30	:30
:45	:45	:45	:45	:45	:45	:45
11	11	11	11	11	11	11
:15	:15	:15	:15	:15	:15	:15
:30	:30	:30	:30	:30	:30	:30
:45	:45	:45	:45	:45	:45	:45
12	12	12	12	12	12	12
:15	:15	:15	:15	:15	:15	:15
:30	:30	:30	:30	:30	:30	:30
:45	:45	:45	:45	:45	:45	:45
1	1	1	1	1	1	1
:15	:15	:15	:15	:15	:15	:15
:30	:30	:30	:30	:30	:30	:30
:45	:45	:45	:45	:45	:45	:45
2	2	2	2	2	2	2
:15	:15	:15	:15	:15	:15	:15
:30	:30	:30	:30	:30	:30	:30
:45	:45	:45	:45	:45	:45	:45
3	3	3	3	3	3	3
:15	:15	:15	:15	:15	:15	:15
:30	:30	:30	:30	:30	:30	:30
:45	:45	:45	:45	:45	:45	:45
4	4	4	4	4	4	4
:15	:15	:15	:15	:15	:15	:15
:30	:30	:30	:30	:30	:30	:30
:45	:45	:45	:45	:45	:45	:45
5	5	5	5	5	5	5
:30	:30	:30	:30	:30	:30	:30
6	6	6	6	6	6	6
:30	:30	:30	:30	:30	:30	:30
7	7	7	7	7	7	7
:30	:30	:30	:30	:30	:30	:30
8	8	8	8	8	8	8
:30	:30	:30	:30	:30	:30	:30
9	9	9	9	9	9	9

Weekly Planner

Tool Defined:

This planner is designed to help you focus on the specific tasks that must be completed within the week. Similar to the Monthly Planner, this tool breaks down your tasks into manageable steps, ensuring that you can allocate your time effectively and stay on track with your weekly intentions.

Origin Story:

I created the Weekly Planner as a way to stay focused on what needed to be accomplished that week. By zeroing in on just one week at a time, I found it easier to prioritize tasks and manage my time.

How I Use It:

I begin with Step 1, where I list out up to 15 tasks that need to be completed this week. For each task, I estimate how much time it will take using the two circles provided next to each item. Each circle represents one hour, so I color in the whole circle if I estimate the task will take an hour, or half the circle for 30 minutes. This helps me get a realistic sense of the time commitment required for each task. On the small line to the left of each task, I identify the best day of the week to get that task done.

In Step 2, I write down all the tasks for each day of the week, cross-referencing with my estimated time for each task. This step is crucial as it allows me to confirm that the total time required for tasks on any given day doesn't exceed the time I have available (represented by time circles in that section).

About the Example:

After listing out my tasks, I estimated the time each would take, with some tasks like "Prep for ADHD-Friendly session" needing about 30 minutes, while others like "Plan podcast episode" required two hours. When I transfer these tasks to the daily breakdown in Part 2, I am able to easily see if I have enough time available to complete the tasks I planned for that day. The line between the time circles indicates a break in the time block. So, on Monday, I can see I have a one-hour block and later that day I have a 3-hour time block.

Make it *YOURS*:

The Weekly To-Dos Planner is all about customizing your week to fit your needs. Play around with the time circles to get a clear visual representation of your weekly tasks, and don't hesitate to shift things around if your original plan seems too packed.

Weekly Planner

Week of: November 6, 2023 **to** November 12, 2023

STEP 1 — WEEKLY To-Dos

Day	Time Est.	To-Do
M	●○	Weekly/Daily Plan
M-Th	●●	Client Prep
M	●●	Plan pod ep. 110
W	●○	Record pod ep. 110
M	◐○	Prep AF plan session

Day:		To-Do
F	●○	Start Planner Slides
Th	●○	Order Table Runner
F	●○	Get Car Serviced
W	●○	Add Dec. events to AF Calendar
Th	●○	Start ASL: 1st line

Day:		To-Do
M-F	●●	Read book club book
M-F	●●	Walk 23 in '23
⇨	○○	Next week: Print AF Event Calendars
	○○	
	○○	

STEP 2 — DAILY To-Dos

Monday
Available Time: ●●●●●
- ● Weekly/Daily Plan
- ●● Plan Podcast 110
- ◐ Prep AF plan session
- ◐ Client Prep
- ◐ Walk 23 in '23
- ◐ Read Book Club Book

Tuesday
Available Time: ●●●●○
- ◐ Client Prep
- ◐ Read Book Club Book
- ◐ Walk 23 in '23

Wednesday
Available Time: ●●●●●
- ◐ Client Prep
- ● Record Podcast Ep. 110
- ● Add Dec. events to AF Calendar
- ◐ Read Book Club Book
- ◐ Walk 23 in '23

Thursday
Available Time: ●●●●●
- ◐ Client Prep
- ● Order table runner
- ● Start ASL: 1st line
- ◐ Read Book Club Book
- ◐ Walk 23 in '23

Friday
Available Time: ●●●○○
- ● Start Planner Slides
- ● Get Car Serviced
- ◐ Read Book Club Book
- ◐ Walk 23 in '23

Sat./Sun.
Available Time: ○○○○○

Next week: Print AF Event Calendars

Patty Blinderman, PCAC, PCC

Weekly Planner

Week of: _____ **to** _____

STEP 1   WEEKLY To-Dos

Day	Time Est.	To-Do	Day:	Day:
___	◯◯	_____	___ ◯◯ _____	___ ◯◯ _____
___	◯◯	_____	___ ◯◯ _____	___ ◯◯ _____
___	◯◯	_____	___ ◯◯ _____	___ ◯◯ _____
___	◯◯	_____	___ ◯◯ _____	___ ◯◯ _____
___	◯◯	_____	___ ◯◯ _____	___ ◯◯ _____

STEP 2   DAILY To-Dos

Monday	Tuesday	Wednesday	Thursday	Friday	Sat./Sun.
Available Time:	Available Time:	Available Time:	Available Time:	Available Time:	Available Time:
◯◯◯◯◯	◯◯◯◯◯	◯◯◯◯◯	◯◯◯◯◯	◯◯◯◯◯	◯◯◯◯◯

    Patty Blinderman, PCAC, PCC

Notes

Patty Blinderman, PCAC, PCC

Daily Planner

Tool Defined:

This tool is designed to help you organize your day with both structure and flexibility. On the right side of the page, you'll find a timeline blocked out from 6 am to 9 pm, allowing you to fill in appointments, meetings, and other time commitments. On the left side, the planner helps you prioritize tasks and capture successes, ensuring that your most important goals are visible.

Origin Story:

I created the Daily Planner because I needed a tool that would do two things: help me see my time for the day and include space to prioritize my top tasks. The simple structure of the planner helps keep me on track throughout the day.

How I Use It:

Each morning, I start by filling in my appointments and time commitments on the right side of the page, so I know exactly when I have open slots to work on my tasks. I also use this space to block off time for errands, meals, and even breaks, ensuring I'm making the best use of my day.

Next, in the box at the top left I fill in up to three important tasks that must get done today. The structure limits me to just three, which helps me focus on what truly matters. These are my non-negotiables for the day, the tasks that, if accomplished, will make me feel successful.

Once my top priorities are identified, I use the box below to list any other tasks that I want to get done after the priorities are complete.

About the Example:

First I filled in the daily schedule and blocked open time in a different color to make it easy to see. Then on the left I identified my top priorities for the day. On this day, I had three key tasks, which went into my top priority box. Other tasks like "plan podcast episode" and "read book club book" were listed in the lower box for later in the day. I also flagged times for meals, exercise, reading, and when I plan to be "done" with work for the day.

Make it *YOURS*:

The Daily Planner is a versatile tool that can be adapted to fit your unique needs. If three priorities feel like too many or too few, adjust the structure to suit your style. Use the timeline to visually map out your day, and don't forget to block time for self-care or unexpected tasks.

Daily Planner

Priorities: Things that must get done	Date: Monday, Nov. 6, 2023

1 ● Weekly/Daily Planning

2 ◑ Prep ADHD-Friendly "Plan your Week" Slides

3 ◑ Prep for session with new client

Things I want to do

●● Plan podcast episode 110

◑ Read Book Club Book (meeting next Monday!)

◔ Walk 23 in 2023

Successes + Notes

Time	
6:00	
6:15	BREAKFAST
6:30	
6:45	
7:00	
7:15	Walk
7:30	
7:45	
8:00	
8:15	1 hour open
8:30	
8:45	
9:00	Client - FT
9:15	
9:30	
9:45	↓
10:00	
10:15	
10:30	
10:45	
11:00	
11:15	3 hours open
11:30	
11:45	
12:00	
12:15	
12:30	
12:45	
1:00	
1:15	LUNCH
1:30	
1:45	
2:00	
2:15	Meeting
2:30	
2:45	
3:00	
3:15	
3:30	
3:45	↓
4:00	
4:15	DONE!
4:30	
4:45	
5:00	
5:15	
5:30	
5:45	
6:00	
6:30	
7:00	
7:30	READ
8:00	
8:30	
9:00	

Daily Planner

Priorities: Things that must get done	Date:
1	6:00
	6:15
	6:30
	6:45
2	7:00
	7:15
	7:30
	7:45
3	8:00
	8:15
	8:30
	8:45
	9:00
Things I want to do	9:15
	9:30
	9:45
	10:00
	10:15
	10:30
	10:45
	11:00
	11:15
	11:30
	11:45
	12:00
	12:15
	12:30
	12:45
	1:00
	1:15
	1:30
	1:45
	2:00
	2:15
	2:30
	2:45
	3:00
	3:15
	3:30
	3:45
	4:00
Successes + Notes	4:15
	4:30
	4:45
	5:00
	5:15
	5:30
	5:45
	6:00
	6:30
	7:00
	7:30
	8:00
	8:30
	9:00

Notes

Patty Blinderman, PCAC, PCC

Stovetop Prioritizer

Tool Defined:

The Stovetop Prioritizer helps you prioritize your tasks by categorizing them into front burner, back burner, simmer, or warming drawer sections. This visual representation makes it easier to see which tasks need immediate attention, which can wait, and which ones should not be forgotten. It's a simple yet effective way to manage your workload and stay organized.

Origin Story:

This tool was inspired by a coaching client who used the front burner and back burner terms when describing the importance of their tasks. Because my brain turns words into pictures, I immediately visualized this tool and created it to support prioritizing tasks. I often find myself overwhelmed by the sheer number of tasks on my to-do list, unsure which to address first. By visualizing my tasks as items on a stovetop, it is easier to distinguish between immediate priorities (front burner) and less urgent tasks (back burner). I use the simmer section for ongoing tasks that need occasional attention, while the warming drawer is for tasks I don't want to forget but don't need immediate action. This tool has helped me focus better and manage my time more effectively.

About the Example:

Front burner tasks in this example are ones that will have a consequence if they are not completed today. For this day, those tasks were paying a bill before it was late and calling to schedule an appointment before the weekend. Back burner tasks I wanted to get done that day, but if I ran out of time, I could put them on the list for the next day. These were less urgent tasks like organizing my files and scheduling a meeting with a colleague. The simmer section had my ongoing project of creating my POM course, while the warming drawer kept reminders for tasks that are upcoming, like renewing my driver's license. I like to use small post-it notes to write my individual tasks on so I can easily move them around, if needed. By using this tool, I am able to reduce my stress and handle my priorities more efficiently.

Make it *YOURS*:

Think about how you can categorize your tasks using the stovetop metaphor. What tasks need to be on your front burner? Which ones can wait on the back burner? What ongoing tasks can you put in the simmer section? And what reminders belong in the warming drawer? If the stovetop layout doesn't work for you, feel free to adapt it to better suit your needs. The goal is to create a system that helps you prioritize effectively and stay organized.

Stovetop Prioritizer

Organize the files on my desk

Back Burner

Schedule a meeting with Jan

Back Burner

Create the POM course

Simmer

Pay electric bill

Front Burner

Schedule doctors appointment

Front Burner

Warming Drawer

Renew driver's license

Stovetop Prioritizer

Back Burner

Back Burner

Simmer

Front Burner

Front Burner

Warming Drawer

Bracket Your Priorities

Tool Defined:

The Bracket Your Priorities tool helps you prioritize your tasks by using a bracket structure similar to the NCAA basketball tournament. Start with a list of 10 tasks on the left, narrow them down to 5 in the middle column, and finalize your top 2-3 priorities on the right. This visual method helps you clear your mind, see all your tasks, and make decisions to whittle down the list, supporting planning, prioritizing, time management, and working memory.

Origin Story:

I created Bracket Your Priorities to support myself at conferences where I often struggled to choose which sessions to attend. By using the bracket structure, I could list all the sessions I was interested in and then narrow them down to my top choices. This tool also helped me remember backup sessions in case my first choice was canceled or too full. This approach made navigating the conference much easier and less stressful, allowing me to make the most of my time and opportunities. Slightly modified here, it now allows me to prioritize my task list with more ease!

About the Example:

This example shows a list of 10 tasks, which were then narrowed down to 5 tasks in the middle column by comparing their urgency and importance. Finally, the top 3 priorities for that day were identified in the brackets on the right. This approach helps to free up space in your mind, prioritize effectively, and manage your time more efficiently.

Make it *YOURS*:

Consider how you can use the bracket structure to prioritize your tasks. List up to 10 tasks on the left side and compare them to narrow down to 5 in the middle. From there, decide on your top 2-3 priorities for the day. If you finish the top three priorities, you can go back to your bracket and see if there is something in the middle section you have time to complete. If the bracket format doesn't fit your style, feel free to adjust it to better suit your needs. The goal is to create a clear, visual system that helps you prioritize and manage your tasks efficiently, supporting your planning, prioritizing, time management, and working memory.

Bracket Your Priorities

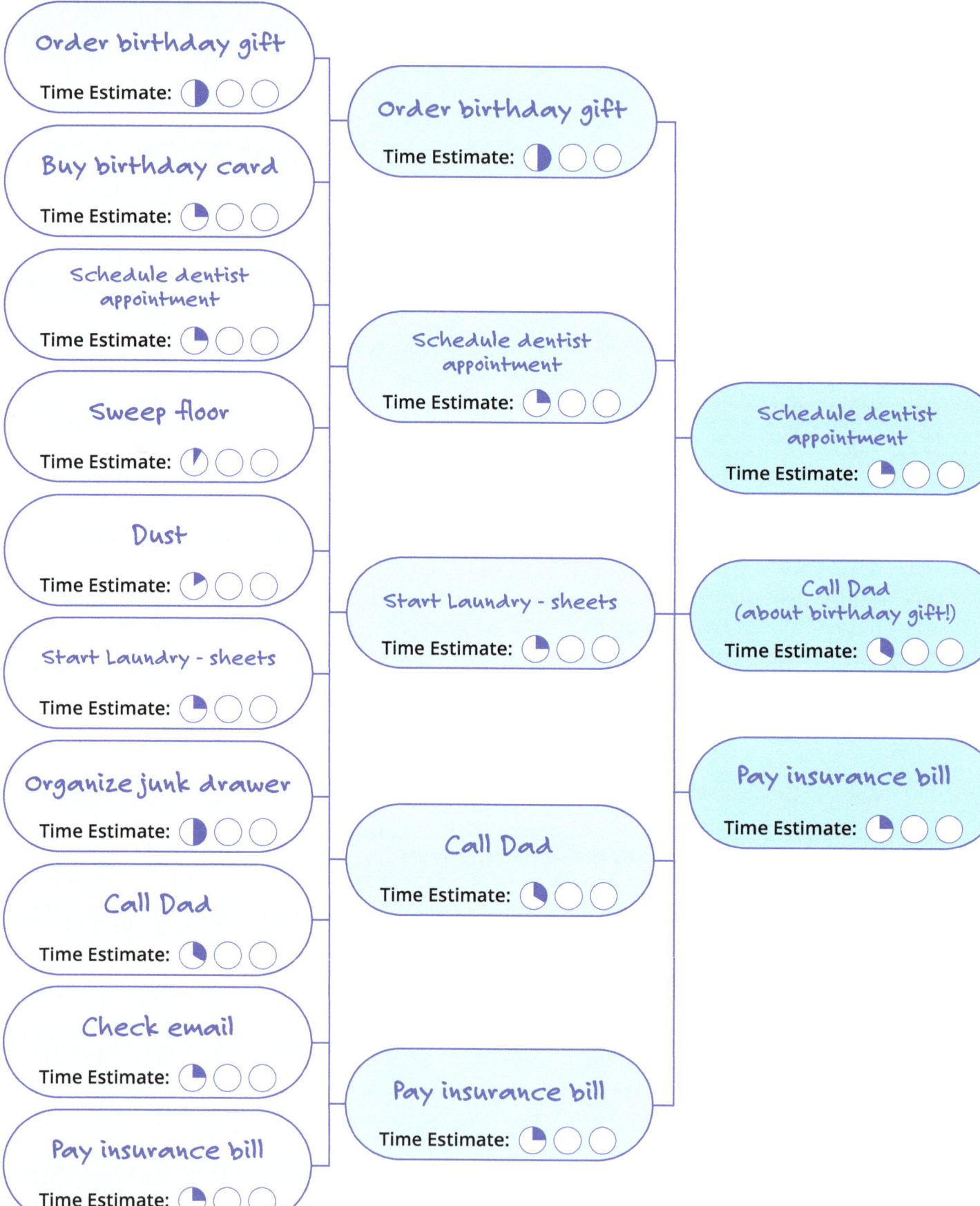

Bracket Your Priorities

Time Estimate: ◯ ◯ ◯

Time Estimate: ◯ ◯ ◯

Time Estimate: ◯ ◯ ◯

Time Estimate: ◯ ◯ ◯

Time Estimate: ◯ ◯ ◯

Time Estimate: ◯ ◯ ◯

Time Estimate: ◯ ◯ ◯

Time Estimate: ◯ ◯ ◯

Time Estimate: ◯ ◯ ◯

Time Estimate: ◯ ◯ ◯

Time Estimate: ◯ ◯ ◯

Time Estimate: ◯ ◯ ◯

Time Estimate: ◯ ◯ ◯

Time Estimate: ◯ ◯ ◯

Time Estimate: ◯ ◯ ◯

Time Estimate: ◯ ◯ ◯

Time Estimate: ◯ ◯ ◯

Notes

5

Task Initiation and the ICNUP Model

Tools:

ICNUP Menu
Rewards Menu

To-Do Menu

Chapter 5

Task Initiation and Getting Started with ADHD

Starting tasks—known as **task initiation**—is one of the biggest challenges for individuals with ADHD. Even when we know what needs to be done, we often find ourselves stuck, unable to take the first step. It's not about being lazy or unmotivated; it's about the way the ADHD brain is wired. Without a clear trigger for urgency or interest, getting started on a task can feel almost impossible. In this chapter, we explore why task initiation is so difficult for those with ADHD and how Dr. William Dodson's **ICNUP model** provides a powerful framework to overcome this barrier. Additionally, we'll introduce three key tools designed to help you get started on tasks and keep the momentum going: the **ICNUP Menu, Rewards Menu,** and **To-Do Menu.**

Why is Task Initiation So Difficult with ADHD?

For those of us with ADHD, initiating a task can feel like pushing a boulder up a hill. Whether it's a simple household chore, a work assignment, or a personal project, there's often an invisible wall that makes starting the task feel overwhelming. This challenge is rooted in the ADHD brain's unique way of processing information and motivation.

Common ADHD-related challenges with task initiation:
- **Executive function deficits:** ADHD impacts the executive function skills that help us break tasks into manageable steps and get started.
- **Lack of internal motivation:** Without a sense of urgency or interest, it's hard to engage with a task.
- **Time blindness:** We may not fully grasp how much time a task will take or how quickly deadlines are approaching, leading to procrastination.
- **Perfectionism or fear of failure:** Starting a task can feel paralyzing if we're afraid of not doing it "right" or getting stuck.

Dr. William Dodson's ICNUP Model: Engaging the ADHD Brain

Dr. William Dodson's **ICNUP model** is a game-changer when it comes to understanding how to engage the ADHD brain. ICNUP stands for **Interest, Challenge, Novelty, Urgency, and Passion**—five elements that can ignite motivation in individuals with ADHD. Essentially, if a task involves one or more of these elements, the ADHD brain is more likely to get started and stay engaged.

Here's how the ICNUP model breaks down:

- **Interest:** Tasks that capture your curiosity or align with your passions are easier to engage with. Finding a personal connection to the task can help you start.

- **Challenge:** If a task presents a difficulty or feels like a puzzle to be solved, it can stimulate the ADHD brain.
- **Novelty:** New and unfamiliar tasks tend to hold our attention more easily, making it simpler to get started.
- **Urgency:** Many people with ADHD rely on deadlines and a sense of urgency to motivate them. When something feels time-sensitive, the adrenaline rush helps us initiate action.
- **Passion:** Dr. Dodson emphasizes that we can't always tap into passion, but when we can, tasks connected to something you care deeply about naturally draw your attention and make it easier to start.

ICNUP is all about using strategies to get your brain engaged in order to initiate tasks.

Tools for Task Initiation

This chapter introduces three practical tools to help you overcome the barrier of starting. These tools are designed to engage the ADHD brain to help you get started with more ease.

1. The ICNUP Menu

The **ICNUP Menu** is a tool designed to help you identify which of the five ICNUP elements—Interest, Challenge, Novelty, Urgency, or Passion—you can apply to a given task. By applying one or more of these elements, you can reframe the task in a way that sparks engagement.

2. The Rewards Menu

Motivation isn't just about getting started; it's also about maintaining momentum. The **Rewards Menu** taps into the ADHD brain's response to incentives by offering rewards for completing tasks. Rewards provide the dopamine boost that keeps you going, even when a task feels difficult or tedious.

By linking each task to a reward, you're creating a powerful motivation loop that encourages task initiation and completion. The ADHD brain thrives on immediate gratification, and this tool allows you to harness that by building in incentives.

3. The To-Do Menu

The **To-Do Menu** is a task management tool inspired by the structure of a restaurant menu. This creative approach breaks tasks into manageable categories: **Appetizers, Main Dishes,** and **Desserts**. Each category serves a specific purpose in helping you initiate and complete tasks while offering rewards to reinforce your progress.

- **Appetizers:** These are small, easy tasks that help you build momentum. Think of them as "warm-ups" that ease you into bigger tasks. For example, answering a quick email, tidying your desk, or making a short phone call.
- **Main Dishes:** These are the priorities for the day—the larger, more important tasks that you need to focus on. Once you've gained momentum from the appetizers, you can dive into these bigger tasks with more confidence.

- **Desserts:** The rewards! After you've completed your main tasks, you get to enjoy the desserts—things that bring you joy and satisfaction. Desserts can be anything from watching your favorite show to going for a walk or indulging in a treat.

The To-Do Menu makes task initiation less daunting by breaking down your day into small steps. Starting with easier "appetizer" tasks helps overcome inertia, while the promise of a reward in the form of "dessert" keeps you motivated to push through the main tasks.

Why These Tools Work for ADHD Brains

All three of these tools—the **ICNUP Menu, Rewards Menu,** and **To-Do Menu**—are designed to align with how the ADHD brain functions. By incorporating elements that naturally engage the brain (such as interest, challenge, and rewards), they make task initiation more manageable. These tools help you work with your ADHD tendencies rather than against them.

- **The ICNUP Menu** helps you reframe tasks by focusing on what stimulates your brain, making starting tasks more appealing.
- **The Rewards Menu** taps into the dopamine-driven nature of the ADHD brain, offering immediate incentives to initiate and complete tasks.
- **The To-Do Menu** creates structure and a sense of progress, making larger tasks feel more manageable and providing small wins along the way.

Conclusion

Starting tasks is one of the most common struggles for those of us with ADHD, but it's also an area where we can make significant improvements with the right tools. In this chapter, we've explored how Dr. William Dodson's **ICNUP model** provides insight into what motivates the ADHD brain and how tools like the **ICNUP Menu, Rewards Menu,** and **To-Do Menu** can help overcome the barrier of task initiation.

By implementing these tools into your daily routine, you'll not only make it easier to get started but also create a sustainable system for keeping yourself engaged and motivated. Task initiation doesn't have to be an insurmountable challenge—these strategies offer a practical, ADHD-friendly approach to help you move from stuck to started.

ICNUP Menu

Tool Defined:
The ICNUP Menu is a tool designed to help engage and energize a brain with ADHD-wiring, based on the ICNUP model by Dr. William Dodson. This tool allows you to capture notes and strategies in the areas of Interest, Challenge/Competition, Novelty/New, Urgency, and *Passion (*sometimes). Using this structure can help define and record personalized strategies to boost engagement.

Origin Story:
Inspired by Dr. William Dodson's approach to ADHD engagement, I created this form to harness his ICNUP model. The acronym stands for:
- **I**nterest
- **C**hallenge/Competition
- **N**ovelty/New
- **U**rgency
- **P**assion (sometimes*)

This tool provides space to jot down notes and strategies for each category. Using this form has helped me pinpoint what gets my brain engaged, and I share it with my clients who are interested in creating their own ICNUP strategies list. Dr. Dodson emphasizes that while passion can be a powerful motivator, it isn't applicable to every task.

About the Example:
The provided example shows various strategies for each of the five categories. Initially, I found myself resistant to using the list, so I customized my version by adding pictures to represent some strategies. Visuals are easier for me to process than text, making the tool more engaging. This visual customization made it more effective for my brain.

With my weak working memory, having a tool that reminds me of energizing strategies is crucial. When struggling to start a task, I'm usually low on energy and creativity. By referring to my ICNUP menu, I often find a strategy to boost my interest and help me get started.

Make it *YOURS*:
- Which ICNUP area is the easiest for you to tap into?
- How could you tweak this tool to make it more accessible for your brain if Task Initiation is an area you struggle with? Consider adding pictures, colors, or other elements that make it more engaging for you.

ICNUP Menu

Task	Interest	Challenge/Competition	Novel/New	Urgency	Passion (Sometimes)
Empty Dishwasher	Top first vs Bottom first	Race the Clock	Audio Book	Race a Kid!	
Refill/Pick Up Rx	Look at steps	Do it first!	Yard Sale	3, 2, 1, GO!	
Write Newsletter and/or Blog	Work with TV on or Whiteboard it!	Track it!	Work on patio	Use Accountability Partner!	Share info to help others
Make Phone Calls	Script	Finish before lunch	Call on business phone	Bet husband $10	
Billpaying/Bookkeeping Tasks	Play energizing music	Beat the Clock	Reward myself!	Schedule Appointment	

Patty Blinderman, PCAC, PCC

ICNUP Menu

Task	Interest	Challenge/Competition	Novel/New	Urgency	Passion (Sometimes)

Patty Blinderman, PCAC, PCC

Rewards Menu

Tool Defined:

The Rewards Menu is a tool designed to help you identify and use incentives to motivate yourself to take action or achieve your goals. It provides a structured way to list and choose rewards that will effectively boost your motivation and help you stay on track.

Origin Story:

When I first started coaching, I encountered a rewards menu that inspired me to create my own version. Although I don't recall the original source, the initial menu wasn't engaging enough for me. Over the years, I've modified the layout and updated many of the reward items to better suit my needs. You might want to customize it similarly to make it work for you!

About the Example:

The completed example provided is my personal rewards menu. I've checked the boxes next to the rewards I want to remember to use when my motivation is low. Additionally, I've added extra rewards in black text that are particularly appealing to me. This customized version helps ensure that I have a go-to list of incentives that truly motivate me.

Make it *YOURS*:

- What would you add or remove to this menu to make it easier to access the rewards that motivate you?
- Think about the types of rewards that excite you. These could be small treats, enjoyable activities, or anything else that feels like a special incentive.
- Customize the layout to make it visually appealing and engaging for you. Consider adding colors, pictures, or other elements that will make the menu more attractive and easier to use.

By tailoring this Rewards Menu to fit your preferences, you'll create a powerful tool that helps you stay motivated and achieve your goals more effectively.

Rewards Menu

Food/Snacks

- ☑ Popcorn
- ☐ Chips
- ☐ Nuts
- ☐ Fruit
- ☐ Candy
- ☑ Ice Cream
- ☑ Chocolate
- ☐ Pizza
- ☐
- ☐

Beverages

- ☐ Hot Cocoa
- ☑ Coffee/Tea
- ☑ Milkshake
- ☐ Smoothie
- ☐ Lemonade
- ☐
- ☐
- ☐
- ☐
- ☐

Exercise

- ☑ Walking
- ☐ Biking
- ☐ Running
- ☐ Gym
- ☐ Swimming
- ☑ Dancing
- ☐ Yoga
- ☐ Pilates
- ☐ Hiking
- ☐

Social

- ☑ Lunch
- ☑ Friend time
- ☐ Texting
- ☐ Social Media
- ☑ Phone Call
- ☐
- ☐
- ☐
- ☐
- ☐

Entertainment

- ☑ Movie
- ☐ YouTube
- ☐ Video game
- ☑ TV Show
- ☑ Reading
- ☑ Puzzles
- ☑ Games
- ☑ Knitting
- ☐
- ☐

Other

- ☐ Camping
- ☑ Shopping
- ☐ Cooking
- ☐ Drawing
- ☐ Volunteer
- ☐ Sewing
- ☑ Baking
- ☐ Stickers
- ☑ Traveling
- ☐

Rewards Menu

Food/Snacks

- ❏ Popcorn
- ❏ Chips
- ❏ Nuts
- ❏ Fruit
- ❏ Candy
- ❏ Ice Cream
- ❏ Chocolate
- ❏ Pizza
- ❏
- ❏

Beverages

- ❏ Hot Cocoa
- ❏ Coffee/Tea
- ❏ Milkshake
- ❏ Smoothie
- ❏ Lemonade
- ❏
- ❏
- ❏
- ❏
- ❏

Exercise

- ❏ Walking
- ❏ Biking
- ❏ Running
- ❏ Gym
- ❏ Swimming
- ❏ Dancing
- ❏ Yoga
- ❏ Pilates
- ❏ Hiking
- ❏

Social

- ❏ Lunch
- ❏ Friend time
- ❏ Texting
- ❏ Social Media
- ❏ Phone Call
- ❏
- ❏
- ❏
- ❏
- ❏

Entertainment

- ❏ Movie
- ❏ YouTube
- ❏ Video game
- ❏ TV Show
- ❏ Reading
- ❏ Puzzles
- ❏ Games
- ❏
- ❏
- ❏

Other

- ❏ Camping
- ❏ Shopping
- ❏ Cooking
- ❏ Drawing
- ❏ Volunteer
- ❏ Sewing
- ❏ Baking
- ❏ Stickers
- ❏
- ❏

Patty Blinderman, PCAC, PCC

To-Do Menu

Tool Defined:

The To-Do Menu is a creative and engaging way to move items on your list from "To-Do" to "Done!" By categorizing tasks like a restaurant menu, this tool helps you prioritize and complete your tasks in a fun and structured manner.

Origin Story:

I have a love/hate relationship with to-do lists. I love creating them, but often struggle to get the items checked off. Sound familiar? As a coach, I enjoy making various "menus" for tools, such as Reward Menus and Energy-Building Menus. During one of my Personal Owner's Manual (POM) Coaching Groups, a member misunderstood a reference to my menu tool, thinking it was an actual restaurant menu. This amusing misunderstanding inspired me to create the To-Do Menu tool, connecting the idea of task management to the structure of a restaurant menu.

About the Example:

This example is taken from my own to-do list and shows how I use the To-Do Menu:

1. **Appetizers/Starters:** I start by looking at my weekly to-do list and picking 1 or 2 small, easy tasks. These "appetizers" are tasks that I can quickly accomplish, giving me early wins that activate my reward center and build momentum. Starting with easy tasks helps me get ready for the bigger "main dishes."
2. **Main Dishes:** Next, I identify the essential tasks for the day. These are the larger, more important items that need to get done but might be prone to procrastination. The momentum from completing the "appetizers" helps me tackle these "main dishes" with more energy and focus.
3. **Desserts:** Finally, I choose my rewards from my Reward Menu. These "desserts" are my favorite part, providing motivation to finish my tasks. Knowing I have a reward waiting makes it easier to start and complete my work.

Notice how starting with smaller "Appetizers" builds up to tackling the larger "Main Dishes" and finally enjoying the "Desserts." This structured approach makes it easier to begin and stay motivated.

Make it *YOURS*:

- What tasks would you choose as your "Appetizers" to help you start more easily?
- What "Main Dishes" are your essential tasks for the day?
- What "Desserts" would work as rewards for you to motivate completion?

Customize the To-Do Menu to fit your preferences and make task management more engaging and enjoyable. By using this tool, you can create a clear, structured path from starting small tasks to completing essential ones, all while enjoying rewards along the way. What "Desserts" would work for you?

To-Do Menu

Appetizers / Starters

Short/Easy Tasks: Check them off and gain some momentum

1. Clear desk of any clutter

2. Client Prep forms

3.

Main Dishes

Today's Essential To-Do's

1. Prepare for new client Intake Session

2. Call about coaching insurance

3.

Desserts

Incentives/Rewards for completing Starters/Main Dishes

1. Check it off the list!

2. Play outside with dogs for 10 minutes

3. If needed: Real dessert (Turtle Sundae!)

4.

5.

To-Do Menu

Appetizers / Starters

Short/Easy Tasks: Check them off and gain some momentum

1.

2.

3.

Main Dishes

Today's Essential To-Do's

1.

2.

3.

Desserts

Incentives/Rewards for completing Starters/Main Dishes

1.

2.

3.

4.

5.

Patty Blinderman, PCAC, PCC

6

Creating an ADHD-Friendly Toolbox

Tools:

Tools & Systems Tracker
Sleep Log
Health Visit Log

Tolerations Worksheet
Must Do Vs Might Do
Blank Menu

Chapter 6

The ADHD-Friendly Toolbox

An essential part of living successfully with ADHD is having the right tools in place to support your unique brain. In this chapter, we'll explore the concept of an **ADHD-Friendly Toolbox**—a personalized collection of go-to tools designed to help you navigate daily challenges. Unlike a one-size-fits-all approach, this toolbox is tailored to your individual needs, strengths, and preferences. The chapter will guide you through identifying which tools work best for you and how to maintain an ongoing system for tracking and refining those tools over time.

Included in this chapter are key tools such as the **Tools and Systems Tracker, Sleep Log, Health Visit Log, Tolerations Worksheet, Must Do vs. Might Do Tool,** and a customizable **Blank Menu** for creating your own personalized routines or systems. These tools are designed to give you flexibility and control over how you manage different aspects of life with ADHD, from health and wellness to task management and emotional regulation.

Why the ADHD-Friendly Toolbox Matters

ADHD is incredibly diverse—what works for one person may not work for another. The **ADHD-Friendly Toolbox** empowers you to discover and collect strategies that help you thrive based on your individual needs. Instead of relying on generic systems that often fall short, the toolbox encourages customization. It becomes a resource that reflects how your brain works, offering tools that fit seamlessly into your life.

Having an ADHD-Friendly Toolbox means:

- **Personalization:** Every brain is different, and so are its needs. Tailor your toolbox specifically to you. It is important to give yourself permission to take what works for you and leave the rest behind. Fill your toolbox with YOUR custom tools!
- **Flexibility:** The tools you use today may evolve as your needs change. The toolbox can grow and adapt with you.
- **Self-awareness:** You gain a deeper understanding of which strategies and systems help you function at your best.
- **Sustainability:** By having a reliable set of go-to tools, you can build sustainable habits that support long-term success.

Tools to Support Your ADHD Toolbox

This chapter introduces six key tools and I invite you to explore which ones you want to add to your ADHD-Friendly Toolbox. As with all tools in the Personal Owner's Manual, they are customizable, flexible tools designed to help you address different areas of life, including task management, health, and tolerations. Let's take a look at each one.

1. Tools and Systems Tracker

The **Tools and Systems Tracker** is an essential part of maintaining an ADHD-friendly lifestyle. ADHD brains often struggle with consistency, so it's important to keep track of the tools and systems you're using, as well as how effective they are over time. This tracker helps you log the different tools you've tried, identify which ones work best for you, and make adjustments as needed.

2. Sleep Log

Sleep can be an ongoing challenge with ADHD. The **Sleep Log** helps you track your sleep patterns, which can impact everything from emotional regulation to task initiation and overall health. ADHD brains often have irregular sleep cycles, making it harder to stick to a consistent schedule. This tool provides a way to monitor and reflect on your sleep habits, making it easier to identify impacts and benefits of sleep.

3. Health Visit Log

Managing ADHD often involves coordinating multiple aspects of healthcare, including therapy, medication, and other health-related appointments. The **Health Visit Log** can help you stay organized and on top of your own, or a loved one's, healthcare needs, which is especially important when dealing with ADHD, as managing appointments and follow-ups can be challenging.

4. Tolerations Worksheet

Tolerations are those small but persistent issues in life that we put up with—like a messy workspace, clutter in your home, or unresolved conflicts—that drain our mental energy. The **Tolerations Worksheet** helps you identify these energy-draining issues and take steps to resolve them.

5. Must Do vs. Might Do Tool

The **Must Do vs. Might Do Tool** is designed to help with task prioritization—one of the executive functions that can be particularly challenging for ADHD brains. This tool helps you separate tasks into two categories: the non-negotiable "Must Dos" and the more flexible "Might Dos." This framework reduces overwhelm and helps you focus on the most critical tasks each day.

6. Blank Menu for Customization

The **Blank Menu** offers a flexible template for creating your own personalized routines, systems, or plans. Just like a restaurant menu offers a variety of options to choose from, the blank menu allows you to fill in categories for meals, exercises, habits, or any other routines that support your ADHD brain.

Conclusion: Building and Maintaining Your ADHD Toolbox

The **ADHD-Friendly Toolbox** is a resource that can support many aspects of your life, from health and wellness to task management and emotional well-being. What makes it so effective is its emphasis on **personalization**—you have the flexibility to choose the tools that work for your brain and your life. And with the help of tracking tools like the **Tools and Systems Tracker**, you can regularly evaluate and refine your toolbox to ensure it continues to meet your needs.

As you work through this chapter, you'll have the opportunity to try out different tools, assess their effectiveness, and customize them to fit your lifestyle. The ADHD-Friendly Toolbox isn't static; it evolves with you, becoming more tailored and effective as you gain deeper insights into what helps you thrive. Whether you're focusing on health, task initiation, tolerations, or all of the above, the toolbox is your go-to resource for building sustainable systems that align with your ADHD brain.

Tools and Systems Tracker

Tool Defined:

This "One-Pager" tool is used to capture all the systems and tools you use to support yourself in one place. Think of it as your personal "toolbox" for managing tasks, staying organized, and evaluating how they are working to support yourself.

Origin Story:

Initially, I created this tool as a working memory aid to keep track of the tools and systems my clients developed during coaching. Without a structured form like this, I am likely to forget details around the systems they are working on. An added benefit of this "toolbox" is that it helps me identify patterns in which tools support them effectively and which do not. After seeing its success with my clients, I started my own to support myself with more ease!

How I Use it:

I use the Tools and Systems Tracker to record the systems and tools I implement. I note what I am working on, how the tool/system worked for me, why I might have stopped using it (if I did), and any tweaks I made to make it more effective. Having this information recorded in a structured format allows me to be more organized and focused. I don't need to rely on my memory to recall what I've tried previously; I simply refer to the Tracker and add any new information.

About the Example:

This example includes entries from my own list. I use basic language to describe the system or tool and I make sure to capture the specific examples or phrases that connect to each tool or system. Having space to record each tool helps me reconnect to them in the future and remember what worked and why I stopped using it, if applicable.

Make it *YOURS*:

- Does the spreadsheet layout work for you, or would a different format be better?
- Is there anything you would want to add to this list to make it more comprehensive?
- I tend to become visually overwhelmed with more than 6 or 7 fields on a spreadsheet. Do you need more fields or fewer?

Customize the Tools and Systems Tracker to fit your needs. The goal is to create a clear and accessible way to track and evaluate the tools and systems that support you. This helps ensure that you have a reliable reference to what works best for you, making it easier to maintain and adapt your strategies over time.

Tools and Systems Tracker

Date Started	Tool/System	Notes/Details	How is this working? (rate 1-10)	What needs to be tweaked?
6/23	Task Initiation Menu	Verbally process; Use accountability partners; Break it into a smaller piece	8	N/A
7/23	Mantras	"Change Expectations to Invitations"; "I can do ANYthing, but I can't do EVERYthing!"	6	Write on post-it and stick on bathroom mirror
7/23	Overwhelm Signs & Triggers	Too many piles (more than 5); Tired/fatigue; Nauseous; Moody/short-tempered; Headache	7	N/A
10/23	Energy Builders	Positive people/Music (Energy Playlist on Spotify)	9	N/A
10/23	Energy Drainers	Negative people; meetings over 90 minutes; not getting 8 hours sleep at least every other night.	10	N/A
1/24	Sleep Hygiene Routine	8:30 pm alarm to prompt awareness of time; PJs, wash face, brush teeth; Listen to audiobook	9	N/A
6/24	Transition Strategies	Block 30 minutes between meetings – process/capture notes; Set time timer to prompt when time to return after a break	10	N/A

Patty Blinderman, PCAC, PCC

Tools and Systems Tracker

Date Started	Tool/System	Notes/Details	How is this working? (rate 1-10)	What needs to be tweaked?

Notes

Patty Blinderman, PCAC, PCC

Sleep Log

Tool Defined:
The Sleep Log is a structured tool to help you track your sleep patterns over the course of a week. It includes prompts to rate your mood, irritability, concentration, focus, energy, motivation, appetite, and impulsivity on a scale of 1-10.

Origin Story:
I created the Sleep Log to gain a better understanding of how my sleep affects different aspects of my daily life. I wanted to see patterns and correlations between my sleep quality and my mood, energy, and overall functioning. By keeping a detailed log, I can make more informed decisions about my sleep habits and identify areas for improvement. I can also use the motivation from the awareness it creates to hold boundaries around my sleep so I am getting the amount I need more consistently.

How I Use it:
Before bed, I record the time I go to sleep. In the morning, I note the time I woke up and the number of hours I slept. Then I rate the quality of my sleep on a scale of 1-10. Throughout the day I use prompts to rate my mood, irritability, concentration, etc. Over time I can review the log to see if there are any patterns or connections between my sleep and my daily ratings.

About the Example:
This example shows one week of a Sleep Log. The blue section on top includes data on sleep and wake times as well as ratings for the overall quality of sleep. Throughout the day, ratings can be added in the green section to capture mood, irritability, concentration, focus, energy, motivation, appetite, and impulsivity. Over time, patterns often become visible. In this example, on days when sleep was poor, ratings for mood and concentration were lower and irritability and impulsivity were higher.

Make it *YOURS*:
- How detailed do you want your Sleep Log to be?
- What additional prompts or questions would help you understand your sleep patterns better?
- Customize the log to fit your needs and preferences, whether it's using +/− ratings instead of numbers, or tracking other factors that might be impacted by your sleep.

If you struggle with sleep, using this tool can make it easier to track and remember your actual sleep patterns, gaining valuable insights into how your sleep impacts your daily life. Awareness of how sleep positively and negatively impacts your day can create motivation and energy to create structure and routines to better support it.

Sleep Log

SLEEP LOG	Fill out each day to track your sleep and its impact on your day.						
Sleep details	**Monday**	**Tuesday**	**Wednesday**	**Thursday**	**Friday**	**Saturday**	**Sunday**
Time I went to sleep (the night before)	11 pm	10:30 pm	11:30 pm	11 pm	10 pm	11 pm	10 pm
# of times I woke up during the night	2	1	3	2	0	1	3
Time I woke up in the morning	6:30 am	7 am	6 am	8 am	6 am	7 am	7 am
Time I got out of bed	7 am	7:15 am	6:45 am	8:15 am	6:15 am	7:30 am	7:15 am
Total time asleep	7.5 hrs	8.5 hrs	6.5 hrs	9 hrs	8 hrs	8 hrs	8 hrs
Overall Quality of Sleep (Scale of 1-10)	6	7	5	7	10	8	7
Symptoms:	Rate the items below. Use a scale of 1 to 10 (1 = AWFUL / 10 = GREAT)						
Concentration	5	7	4	7	9	8	7
Memory	7	8	5	7	8	7	8
Focus	5	7	4	8	8	9	6
Energy Level	5	6	3	6	10	8	6
Mood	6	5	4	6	9	10	8
Irritability	6	5	4	7	8	8	7
Motivation	4	6	4	5	10	8	6
Task Initiation	4	5	3	6	8	7	7
Task Completion	5	6	4	5	7	7	6
Impulsivity	5	7	5	7	9	9	8
Procrastination	4	6	4	7	9	7	6
Flexibility	6	5	4	8	10	8	7
Other:							
NOTES:			I felt so sluggish all day :(		Wish I could sleep like this every night!	I got so much done today!	

Patty Blinderman, PCAC, PCC

Sleep Log

SLEEP LOG	Fill out each day to track your sleep and its impact on your day.						
Sleep details	Monday	Tuesday	Wednesday	Thursday	Friday	Saturday	Sunday
Time I went to sleep (the night before)							
# of times I woke up during the night							
Time I woke up in the morning							
Time I got out of bed							
Total time asleep							
Overall Quality of Sleep (Scale of 1-10)							
Symptoms:	Rate the items below. Use a scale of 1 to 10 (1 = AWFUL / 10 = GREAT)						
Concentration							
Memory							
Focus							
Energy Level							
Mood							
Irritability							
Motivation							
Task Initiation							
Task Completion							
Impulsivity							
Procrastination							
Flexibility							
Other:							
NOTES:							

Patty Blinderman, PCAC, PCC

Notes

Health Visit Log

Tool Defined:

The Health Visit Log is a structured tool designed to support you during medical appointments. It includes space to note the date, doctor you are seeing, blood pressure (BP), weight, and other vital statistics. Additionally, it has sections for recording questions you want to remember to ask, the doctor's answers, and any diagnoses, prescriptions, or directions provided by the doctor.

Origin Story:

I created this Health Visit Log after realizing I often forgot to ask important questions during my medical appointments and struggled to remember the doctor's instructions afterward. By using this log, I can ensure I have a comprehensive record of each visit, helping me manage my health more effectively and stay on top of my medical care.

How I Use it:

Before each medical appointment, I fill out the section with the date and the name of the doctor I'm seeing. I make a list of questions I want to ask during the visit. During the appointment, I use the log to record my blood pressure, weight, and any other vital statistics noted by the doctor. As the doctor answers my questions, I write down their responses. I also note any diagnosis, prescriptions, and directions given by the doctor.

About the Example:

This example shows you might use the Health Visit Log to support a pediatric appointment for one of your children. Notice the date, the doctor's name, blood pressure, height and weight are noted. There are three examples of questions that might be forgotten if not written down. Examples of responses are quickly captured, as well as an example of a new diagnosis, a prescription for medication, and specific directions for follow-up care. Having this detailed record allows you to leave appointments feeling confident you asked the questions you needed answered and captured any details you didn't want to forget.

Make it *YOURS*:

- What additional sections would make this log more useful for you?
- Do you need more space for questions and answers, or would you prefer to track other health metrics?
- Customize the log to fit your unique health needs, ensuring it supports you in making the most of your medical appointments.

By consistently using the Health Visit Log, you can have a clear and organized record of your medical visits, helping you stay informed and proactive about your health care.

Patty Blinderman, PCAC, PCC

Health Visit Log

Name: Sara Baker

Date: 8/1/24   **Doctor/Location:** Samuels; Main Street

Height: 48.5"   **Weight:** 51 lbs.   **BP:** 90/60   **Temp:** 98.2

Current Prescriptions:
N/A

Reason for Appointment/Symptoms:
Annual Physical

Questions to ask:
- ☑ Possible ADHD? Yes. Questionnaires for me and pre-school teachers
- ☑ Sleep schedule- naps still needed? Continue offering quiet time
- ☑ New mole? Skin tag. Nothing needs to be done.

Diagnosis/Feedback:
N/A

Directions from Doctor:
1. Complete my ADHD questionnaire
2. Give teachers their questionnaires to complete
3. Return in 1 month for follow-up on possible ADHD diagnosis

Prescriptions/Tests ordered:
N/A

Notes:
Offer quiet time in the afternoon, read, rest, but don't expect sleep.

Health Visit Log

Name: _____

Date: _____ **Doctor/Location:** _____

Height: _____ **Weight:** _____ **BP:** _____ **Temp:** _____

Current Prescriptions:

_____

Reason for Appointment/Symptoms:

_____

_____

Questions to ask:

☐ _____

☐ _____

☐ _____

Diagnosis/Feedback:

_____

Directions from Doctor:

1. _____

2. _____

3. _____

Prescriptions/Tests ordered:

_____

_____

Notes:

Notes

Patty Blinderman, PCAC, PCC

Tolerations Worksheet

Tool Defined:

Tolerations, by definition, are things that drain your energy. The Tolerations Worksheet is a tool to help you identify and manage the things you are tolerating in your life, from minor annoyances like a lightbulb that needs changing to larger issues like the check engine light in your car. Once on your list, you can then use specific strategies, called the 8 D's (listed below), to address them.

Origin Story:

I learned about the 7 Ds to help eliminate tolerations while in my coach training program. When I used them to support myself, I realized I needed more structure so I created the Tolerations Worksheet. After realizing how much energy I was losing to tolerations involving other people, I added an 8th D to my toleration-busting strategy: Discuss. By listing my tolerations in a spreadsheet format, I could see just how much they were impacting me.

How I Use it:

I start by making a comprehensive list of all the things I'm tolerating. Once the list is complete, I go through each item and apply one or more of the 8 Ds to address it. Here's how the 8 Ds work:

- **Do:** Take action and complete the task.
- **Delete:** Remove the item from your list (if feasible).
- **Decide:** Make a decision about what to do with the item.
- **Delegate:** Assign the task to someone else to complete.
- **Divide:** Break the task into smaller, more manageable pieces.
- **Discuss:** Talk through the issue with the person involved to address and resolve it.
- **Due Date:** Assign a deadline to ensure the task gets done.
- **Deal with:** Accept the situation, especially if it can't be changed, as with a chronic illness.

About the Example:

I listed a range of tolerations, and for each item I applied one of the 8 Ds. For instance, I Did change the lightbulb, Delegated the car maintenance to my husband, and Decided to create a plan for scheduling an annual physical with a new doctor, breaking it down into manageable steps (Divide). For a recurring issue with a family member's comments, planning to Discuss this over a coffee date was the best way forward.

Make it *YOURS*:

- What types of tolerations are draining your energy the most?
- Which of the 8 Ds will be most helpful for you to address each toleration?
- Customize the worksheet to fit your needs, and consider adding categories or strategies that resonate with you.

By regularly using the Tolerations Worksheet, you can systematically reduce the energy drain from tolerations in your life, making it easier to focus on what truly matters and maintain your overall well-being.

Tolerations Worksheet

TOLERATION	Do	Decline/ Delete	Decide	Delegate	Divide	Discuss	Due Date	Deal with it (accept)
change flickering lightbulb	✓							
check engine light				✓				
find a new doctor			✓		✓			
Brenda's passive aggessive comments						✓		

Tolerations Worksheet

TOLERATION	Do	Decline/ Delete	Decide	Delegate	Divide	Discuss	Due Date	Deal with it (accept)

Patty Blinderman, PCAC, PCC

Notes

Patty Blinderman, PCAC, PCC

Must Do Vs Might Do

Tool Defined:

The Must Dos vs. Might Dos tool is a simple yet effective prioritization tool designed to help you focus on what absolutely needs to be done (Must Dos) while keeping less urgent tasks (Might Dos) accessible but not distracting. The tool features two columns: the left column for Must Dos and the right column for Might Dos, separated by a dotted line. When you fold the page in half, only the Must Dos are visible, supporting you to stay focused on your top priorities.

Origin Story:

I first used the Must Dos vs. Might Dos tool after struggling to prioritize my daily tasks effectively. Often, I found myself overwhelmed by a long to-do list that mixed essential and non-essential tasks. By separating tasks into Must Dos and Might Dos, I could focus on what really needed to get done without getting sidetracked by less critical activities.

How I Use it:

To use the Must Dos vs. Might Dos tool, start by listing your tasks for the day in the appropriate columns:

- **Must Dos:** These are the tasks that are critical to complete today. They are your top priorities and need your immediate attention.
- **Might Dos:** These are tasks that are not as urgent. They can be addressed if you have extra time after completing your Must Dos.

Once you have your tasks listed, fold the page along the dotted line to hide the Might Dos column. This way, you can concentrate on your Must Dos without distraction, while knowing that your Might Dos are still accessible if you have time to tackle them or need to add something else to that list.

About the Example:

Must Dos for this day included preparing a presentation for my membership community, prepare for a scheduled meeting, and completing a speaker agreement that was due by the end of the day. Might Dos included tasks like organizing my desk, replying to non-urgent emails, and brainstorming ideas for a future project. By folding the page, I focused solely on my Must Dos, supporting myself to focus on the critical tasks.

Make it *YOURS*:

- What criteria do you use to determine your Must Dos?
- How do you decide which tasks can go on the Might Dos side?
- Customize the tool, perhaps using it for weekly tasks vs. daily, etc.

By regularly using the Must Dos vs. Might Dos tool, you can maintain a clear focus on your top priorities, reducing stress and increasing productivity. This simple yet powerful method helps you stay on track with what truly matters, while still keeping lesser tasks within reach.

MUST DO	**Might DO**
• Practice presentation	• organize desk
• Prep for 3 pm meeting	• reply to non-urgent emails
• complete speaker agreement (due by the end of day)	• brainstorm ideas for next project.

MUST DO | *Might DO*

Patty Blinderman, PCAC, PCC

Patty Blinderman, PCAC, PCC

Blank Menu

Tool Defined:

The Blank Menu is a tool for you to customize your own menu of options.

Origin Story:

I always have a blank menu handy. It is a place where I can capture ideas when I think of a new tool that will support me. I have menus for exercising, clothes (what to wear depending on the weather or occasion), rewards, chores (by time required to do them), energy-building activities, and more.

About the Example:

This is one of my exercise menus. I have struggled on and off to build a consistent exercise habit. Having a "menu" of options allows me to get out of "all or nothing" thinking and just do something. I like to identify different activities for different weather or the amount of time needed to do them. Because I have recorded these options, if I need to exercise but can't do what I initially planned for any reason, I don't have to think about what else I could do. I simply look at my menu and choose what is appealing to me at that time.

Make it *YOURS*:

- What type of menu is engaging enough for you to begin adding to it?
- Remember, you don't need to complete it in one sitting. Just having the structure allows you to return to it and continue adding strategies that work for you over time!

Customize your Blank Menu to fit your needs. Whether it's for exercise, daily chores, or any other area of your life, this tool helps you avoid "all or nothing" thinking and encourages you to take action by providing a variety of options to choose from.

Blank Menu

Inside
- Yoga video
- Treadmill
- Dumbells
- Stairs

Outside
- Running
- Walking
- Gardening/Yard work

Quick & Easy
- Stairs
- Walk
- Stretches
- Lunges/Crunches

$
- Gym membership
- Personal Trainer
- Online classes

Exercise Menu

30-60 min
- Walk/Run
- Yoga/Pilates video

Social
- Walk/run with a friend
- Treadmill/call a friend
- Meetup Running Group

Sparkly
- Reward after
- New workout accessory

When in a slump...
- Track workouts
- Register for event (.5 marathon)
- Accountability partners

Patty Blinderman, PCAC, PCC

Menu

Patty Blinderman, PCAC, PCC

7

Know Thyself

Tools:

Cheat Sheet for Working with Me
ADHD Success Puzzle
Top 5 Tolerations

Energy Builders & Drainers
Exercise Menu
Resistance Busters

Know Thyself – Tools for Growing Self-Awareness

The final chapter of the Personal Owner's Manual (POM) brings together tools that focus on one of the most essential aspects of living well with ADHD: knowing yourself. Self-awareness, or **metacognition**, is about understanding your patterns, strengths, weaknesses, and what truly works for you. Without this awareness, it can be difficult to manage the day-to-day challenges of ADHD. Chapter 7 provides practical tools that help you deepen this understanding and apply it in ways that support your success.

These "Know Thyself" tools are all about increasing your awareness of how you function best, what drains your energy, and what builds it. By using these tools, you'll gain clarity on your own needs and preferences, allowing you to make more informed decisions and set yourself up for success.

Included in this chapter are:
- **Cheat Sheet for Working with Me**
- **Top 5 Tolerations Tool**
- **ADHD Success Puzzle**
- **Exercise Menu**
- **Energy Builders and Drainers Tool**
- **Resistance Busters**

The Importance of Knowing Yourself

For people with ADHD, understanding how your brain works, what motivates you, and what derails you, is critical to designing a life that fits your unique needs. Traditional approaches often overlook these personal preferences, but the Know Thyself tools provide a framework for identifying your patterns.

Knowing yourself means understanding:
- **Your energy cycles:** When do you feel most energized? What drains you?
- **What motivates you:** What are the tasks, environments, people, and activities that engage your brain and make it easier to stay on track?
- **What creates resistance:** What are the barriers or mental blocks that make starting tasks, on staying on- task, difficult?
- **Your needs and preferences:** What environments, systems, or supports help you thrive?

Tools to Know Thyself

In this chapter, we introduce six tools designed to help you grow your self-awareness and better understand your ADHD brain.

1. Cheat Sheet for Working with Me

The **Cheat Sheet for Working with Me** is a tool that allows you to clarify for yourself what works best for you and/or to communicate your needs and preferences to others. Whether you're using this to support yourself or sharing it with colleagues, family members, or friends, it is a quick reference guide that outlines the environment and conditions that support you to work at your best.

2. Top 5 Tolerations Tool

Much like the Tolerations Worksheet from earlier, the **Top 5 Tolerations Tool** focuses on identifying the most significant issues that are draining your energy in your life in three areas: at home, at work, and/or in your family/community. These are the big tolerations—the persistent problems or annoyances that, when left unchecked, can sap your ability to function at your best. Using this tool can help you identify patterns in your tolerations and maybe even get them checked off more easily!

3. ADHD Success Puzzle

The **ADHD Success Puzzle** is a visual tool that lets you identify individual "pieces" that when used together create the elements that contribute to your success. It can be used to support morning, evening or other routines. It encourages you to check off pieces as you complete them in order to signify "wins" that often go unnoticed but are critical to building momentum.

4. Exercise Menu

The **Exercise Menu** is a customizable tool that allows you to create a menu of physical activities that you enjoy and that suit your energy levels. Regular exercise can have a significant positive impact on ADHD symptoms, including improving focus, mood, and energy regulation. This tool is designed to support creating a menu to make it easier to check off your exercise goals!

5. Energy Builders and Drainers Tool

The **Energy Builders and Drainers Tool** is all about identifying what gives you energy and what takes it away. ADHD brains often struggle to regulate energy, so it is important to be aware of the factors that contribute to both.

6. Resistance Busters

Resistance Busters are questions designed to help you overcome the barriers that make it difficult to start tasks. ADHD brains often struggle with task initiation, and feelings of resistance can get in the way of productivity. This tool helps you break through that resistance by asking yourself questions to "coach" yourself to identify obstacles and what step/s will help you to get started.

Conclusion: Growing Self-Awareness

The tools in this chapter are designed to help you cultivate a deeper understanding of yourself and your ADHD brain. The more you know about what works for you, the more control you'll have over your life. These tools aren't just about managing ADHD; they're about **empowering** you to live in a way that honors your unique strengths, preferences, and needs.

As you continue to build and refine your **Personal Owner's Manual**, these "Know Thyself" tools will be essential in helping you make informed decisions, manage your energy, and support your success. The journey of self-awareness is ongoing, and these tools are here to guide you along the way.

Cheat Sheet for Working with Me

Tool Defined:
This is a personalized tool that supports yourself and others to understand how to best interact with you. Inspired by a business tool, it's valuable in any area where clear communication is key. It outlines your working preferences, communication style, and ideal conditions for productivity.

Origin Story:
After seeing a business worksheet that asked questions to determine how a person best communicates with others, I created this tool that allows you to express your needs clearly, improving understanding and cooperation in both professional and personal settings.

How I Use it:
Complete these prompts to outline preferences:
- **Best Time of Day:** Identify when you're most productive (e.g., late morning).
- **Preferred Communication Style:** Specify your favorite methods (e.g., written communication like email, or in-person meetings).
- **Feedback Preference:** Indicate how you like to receive feedback (e.g., written first, then discussed).

Capturing this information helps you remember your best work environment and productive times, and can be a collaborative tool to use with others, when appropriate, in order to share your preferences and enhance collaboration.

About the Example:
- **Best Time of Day:** Late morning, around 10 AM to noon.
- **Preferred Communication Style:** Email for most matters; in-person for complex issues.
- **Feedback Preference:** Written first, with an option for follow-up discussion. No feedback in a group setting; one-on-one is best.
- **Environment:** Quiet, soft lighting, neat and organized.
- **What I Need to Thrive:** Accountability; To doodle during meetings to support my focus.

Make it *YOURS*:
- What are your non-negotiables when working with others?
- Customize this tool to reflect your unique needs.

This tool helps you advocate for yourself and ensures others know how to support you effectively.

Cheat Sheet for Working with Me

The best time of day for me to get things done

Late morning, around 10 AM to noon.

The best way for people to communicate with me is...

Email for most matters; in-person for complex issues.

How I like to get feedback...

Written first, with an option for follow-up discussion.
No feedback in a group setting; one-on-one is best.

The environment I am most productive in...

Quiet, soft lighting, neat and organized.

What I Need to Thrive

Accountability; To doodle during meetings to support my focus.

Cheat Sheet for Working with Me

The best time of day for me to get things done

The best way for people to communicate with me is...

How I like to get feedback...

The environment I am most productive in...

What I Need to Thrive

Patty Blinderman, PCAC, PCC

Patty Blinderman, PCAC, PCC

ADHD Success Puzzle

Tool Defined:

As important as it is to capture successes, it is also essential to understand what pieces are necessary to support you in having more of them. That is the inspiration behind the ADHD Success Puzzle. It is designed to not only identify the individual components of your successes, but also to keep them in sight so you remember them throughout your day.

Origin Story:

Jigsaw puzzles are one of my favorite ways to include play in my day. I used the puzzle structure to create a tool that gamifies supporting myself! By observing the components that go into making my successes possible, I notice trends and turn them into puzzle pieces.

How I Use It:

On days where I need more structure to get going, I pull out my ADHD Success Puzzle and add the "pieces" needed to support me that day.

About the Example:

Two of the four puzzles are filled-in with examples of the "pieces" or elements that might lead to more successes. The first example includes elements that contribute to a "Balanced Day." The second example includes the pieces of my morning routine that launch my day in a positive way.

Make it *YOURS*:

Your puzzle can illustrate your most successful morning routine, a way to sustain your energy and focus throughout the day, or a sleep hygiene routine to support your getting more restorative sleep, etc.

If you want to try this tool, the first step is to identify YOUR puzzle pieces.
  • Make a list of what you have observed to be the main elements in your successes – your important puzzle pieces.

Fill in a blank puzzle with the elements you identified and color in the individual pieces as you complete those actions. Each puzzle piece you color is like checking an item off a list. It serves as a reward!

This puzzle can be used as a tool to support a successful morning, day, project, or other area of your life.

ADHD Success Puzzle

Identify the key "pieces" that make up your unique puzzle.
Color them in as you use them to support yourself throughout the day.

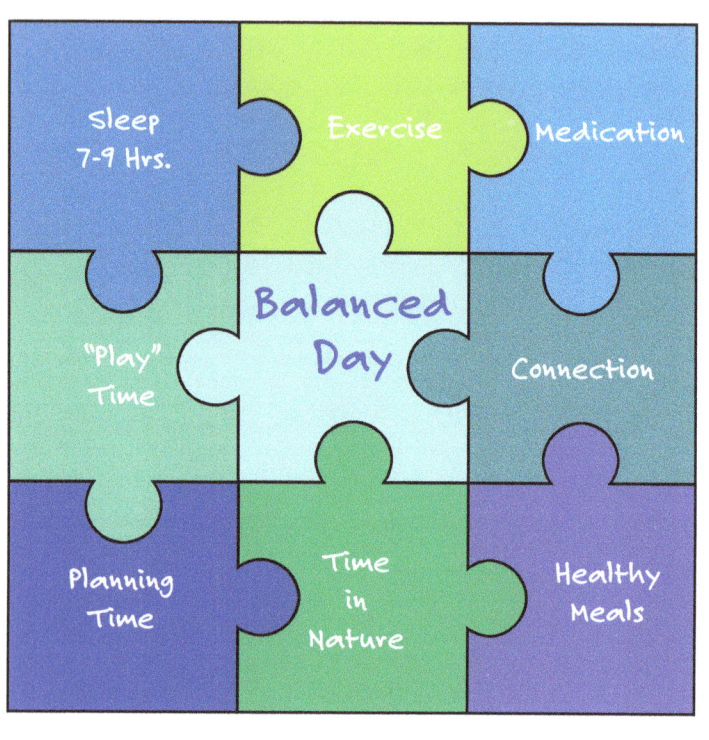

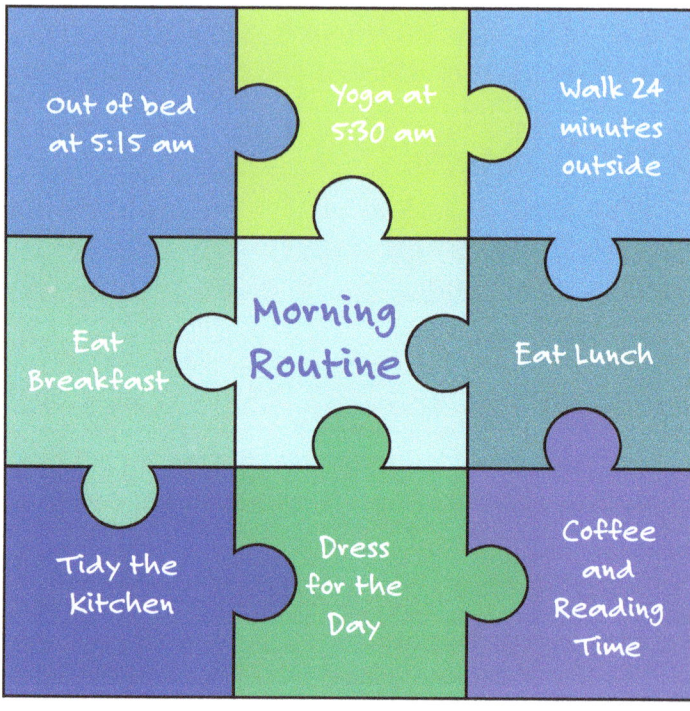

Identify the key "pieces" that make up your unique puzzle.
Color them in as you use them to support yourself throughout the day.

Notes

Top 5 Tolerations

Tool Defined:

The Top 5 Tolerations tool is designed to help individuals identify and address the top things they're tolerating in three key areas: home, work, and family/community. By listing these tolerations and analyzing patterns, you can begin taking steps to resolve them using structured prompts.

Origin Story:

I created this tool while leading a training for ADHD Coaches, aiming to provide them with a structured way to support their clients in identifying and addressing their top tolerations. This tool offers a clear framework to help users recognize and systematically address the things that drain their energy, allowing them to regain focus and productivity.

How I Use It:

I use this tool by first listing up to five things I'm tolerating in each area—home, work, and family/community. For example, at home, my tolerations might include a burnt-out lightbulb, dirty floors, and piles of papers. Once I have my lists, I look for patterns in each area, noting common themes or recurring issues. This helps me to see what's contributing most to my stress. Finally, I use the prompts at the bottom of the tool, tied back to the 8 Ds (Do, Decide, Divide, Due Date, Delegate, Delete, Discuss, Deal with), to take actionable steps in addressing these tolerations.

About the Example:

In the home section, if my top tolerations include a cluttered kitchen, laundry that's piling up, and piles of paper on the counter, I might notice a pattern of visual clutter. Recognizing this pattern allows me to focus on creating a plan to tackle the clutter, and to use the 8 Ds to delegate them, set a due date to complete them, or do them myself.

Make it *YOURS*:

Customize the tool to reflect your own tolerations. Begin by listing the top five tolerations in each area, then look for patterns that may reveal underlying issues. Use the 8 Ds at the bottom of the tool to guide your next steps. This tool can help you systematically reduce the things that drain your energy and create more space for what matters most.

Top 5 Tolerations

At Home

Identify five items you are tolerating (whether or not you have a solution).
Ex: Where are you living; the amount of storage available; small kitchen; high mortgage/taxes; carpet stains; broken appliance, etc.

1. Lightbulb out in kitchen
2. Floors are dirty
3. Coffee table cluttered
4. Car needs to be washed
5. Pictures all over DR table

What patterns are there?

All are things I can see: Visual clutter/dirt/lighting

At Work

Identify five things you are tolerating in your work or professional life (whether or not you have a solution).
Ex: Difficult boss, low pay, work hours, commute, boring work, responsibilities, etc.

1. Slides need to be created
2. Desk is cluttered
3. Proposal outline not done
4. Future direction unknown
5. Website not finished yet

What patterns are there?

All are things that need to be done or require decisions

In your Family/Community

Identify five items you are tolerating in your family/community (whether or not you have a solution).
Ex: Friend's judgment, loud neighbors, spouse habitually late, children not picking up after themselves, etc.

1. No social plans on cal.
2. Kids not helping w/ house
3. Neighbor's kids loud
4. Negative friend
5. Family impulsivity

What patterns are there?

Mostly tolerating negative emotions (loud, negative, etc.)

What can I DO, DIVIDE, DECIDE, or set a DUE DATE for?

DO: Change lightbulb (3 min.)
   Put pictures in one bin
Decide: Make plans for lunch with Lisa
Divide: tasks for kids to help with

What can I DELEGATE, DELETE, DISCUSS, or DEAL WITH (accept)?

Delegate: Car wash (kid) ; wash floors (kid)
Delete: Coffee table (cross off. Can do in future
Deal with/accept: neighbors kids; family impulsivity
Discuss: Talk with friend

Patty Blinderman, PCAC, PCC

Top 5 Tolerations

At Home

Identify five items you are tolerating (whether or not you have a solution).
Ex: Where are you living; the amount of storage available; small kitchen; high mortgage/ taxes; carpet stains; broken appliance, etc.

1.

2.

3.

4.

5.

What patterns are there?

At Work

Identify five things you are tolerating in your work or professional life (whether or not you have a solution).
Ex: Difficult boss, low pay, work hours, commute, boring work, responsibilities, etc.

1.

2.

3.

4.

5.

What patterns are there?

In your Family/Community

Identify five items you are tolerating in your family/ community (whether or not you have a solution).
Ex: Friend's judgment, loud neighbors, spouse habitually late, children not picking up after themselves, etc.

1.

2.

3.

4.

5.

What patterns are there?

What can I DO, DIVIDE, DECIDE, or set a DUE DATE for?

What can I DELEGATE, DELETE, DISCUSS, or DEAL WITH (accept)?

Patty Blinderman, PCAC, PCC

Notes

Energy Builders & Drainers

Tool Defined:

The Energy Builders & Drainers tool is designed to help you identify activities, environments, and situations that either boost or deplete your energy. By becoming more aware of these factors, you can strategically use energy builders to recharge when you're low and limit or prepare for situations that drain your energy. This tool helps you manage your energy levels more effectively, ensuring you have the fuel needed to get through your day.

Origin Story:

I created the Energy Builders & Drainers tool when I realized that when I was low energy, asking myself to think of something to recharge was impossible. By having a list of activities in my Personal Owner's Manual, I can tap into them with ease when they are needed. This tool has become a vital part of my self-care routine, helping me maintain a more consistent energy level and preventing burnout.

How I Use It:

I use this tool to capture situations that build and drain my energy. On the left I list activities or situations that build my energy and on the right side, I note what drains my energy.

About the Example:

Energy Builders & Drainers example lists "Energy Builders" like taking a walk outside, practicing yoga, having a meaningful conversation with a friend, listening to uplifting music, or working on a creative project. On the "Energy Drainers" side, examples include clutter, crowded spaces, noisy environments, and hot weather.

Make it *YOURS*:

Tailor the Energy Builders & Drainers tool to reflect your unique preferences and lifestyle. Everyone has different activities and situations that affect their energy levels, so it's important to personalize this tool. You might find that certain activities are both builders and drainers depending on the context—for example, socializing might energize you in small groups but drain you in large ones. Use this tool to create a customized energy management plan that supports you to navigate your day with greater ease.

Energy Builders & Drainers

taking a walk outside

clutter

practicing yoga

crowded spaces

having a meaningful conversation with a friend

noisy environments

listening to uplifting music

hot weather

working on a creative project

Patty Blinderman, PCAC, PCC

Energy Builders & Drainers

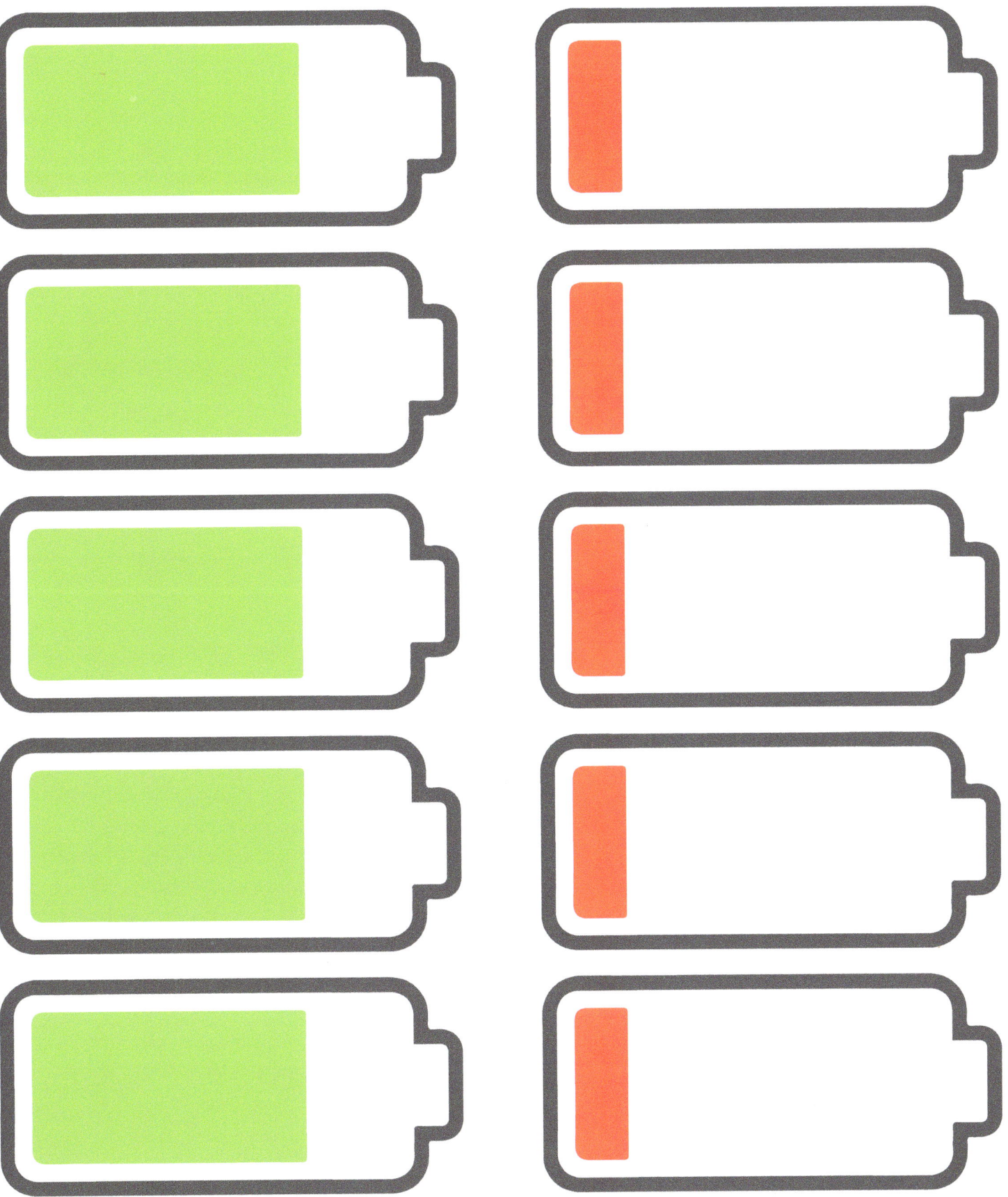

Notes

Exercise Menu

Tool Defined:

The Exercise Menu is an ADHD-Friendly tool designed to help you capture and organize exercises that work best for you. With space to categorize different types of exercises and list specific routines or activities under each, this tool makes it easy to see all your exercise options at a glance, helping you choose what's most appealing or suitable on any given day.

Origin Story:

I created the Exercise Menu as a way to break through my resistance to getting started on my exercise intention. Like many people, I found myself struggling to maintain a consistent exercise habit. This tool allows me to categorize and diversify my workouts, giving me a range of options that fit different moods, energy levels, and time constraints. Whether I want a quick yoga session, a brisk walk, or a more intense cardio workout, my Exercise Menu is my go-to guide.

How I Use It:

I use the Exercise Menu to keep track of various exercises that I enjoy or find effective. The tool has space for five different categories of exercise, such as Yoga, Walking, Weight-Bearing, Cardio, etc. Under each category, I list specific activities or routines. For example, under "Yoga," I might list routines like "Morning Stretch" or "Vinyasa Flow." In the "Cardio" category, I could include activities like running, tennis, or pickleball. Having these options written down helps me quickly decide on an exercise based on how much time I have or what the weather is like outside.

About the Example:

Categories included are: Yoga, with specific routines; Walking, with notes on different trails or routes I like; Weight-Bearing exercises like planks, pushups, and dumbbells; Cardio, featuring running, tennis, and pickleball; and Social Exercises, such as pickleball and dancing. This structure allows me to pick an exercise that fits my current needs, whether I want to work out alone or with others, or choose between an exercise that is low-impact or high-energy. Because I am very visual, I added images to represent most of the options in my menu.

Make it *YOURS*:

Customize the categories and exercises on your menu to reflect what works best for you. Whether you prefer solo workouts or social activities, high-intensity cardio or gentle yoga, this tool can be tailored to fit your lifestyle and preferences.

Exercise Menu

WALK 	YOGA 	WEIGHTS 	SWEAT 	With Others 
Small or Long Loop	Breathe: Day 9 22 min. Balance	Dumbbells 	Run 	Walk 
Lake	Breathe Day 18 30 min. Savor	Planks 	Tennis 	Pickleball 
Forest Preserve	Breathe: Day 24 22 min. Process (great balance)	Pushups 	Pickleball 	Dancing 
Library Paths	Flow: Day 9 23 min. Release	Resistance Bands 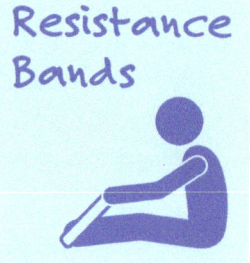	Dancing 	
Walking Trails	Flow: Day 15 22 min. Balance	Lunges/ Stairs 		

Patty Blinderman, PCAC, PCC

Exercise Menu

Notes

Resistance Busters

Tool Defined:

The Resistance Busters tool is designed to help you break through the barriers that keep you from completing tasks on your to-do list. This tool focuses on three common types of resistance: unknowns, low motivation, and stress or fear. By identifying which type of resistance is at play, you can pinpoint the specific challenge keeping you stuck and develop a solution or action step to overcome it.

Origin Story:

I developed the Resistance Busters tool after noticing that certain tasks lingered on my to-do list. Even when I knew a task was important, something seemed to hold me back from starting or completing it. I realized that understanding the root cause of this resistance was key to moving forward. Often it was as simple as not knowing a phone number to make a call or clarifying what "done" looked like. By creating a structured way to identify and address the resistance, I was able to make progress on tasks that had previously felt insurmountable.

How I Use It:

When I notice that I'm avoiding a particular task, I turn to the Resistance Busters tool to identify what's holding me back. I first determine whether the resistance is due to unknowns, low motivation, or stress/fear (or a combination of these!). For each category, there are targeted questions to help me dig deeper into the issue. Once I've identified the specific challenge, I write my answers in the corresponding column. Finally, I brainstorm a solution or an action step to address the resistance and jot it down in the last column.

About the Example:

For example, I used the Resistance Busters tool when I found myself struggling to start work on my TADD Talk for ADDA. I realized that one of my biggest obstacles was not knowing when the deadline was, which created a sense of uncertainty and made it hard to get motivated. By using the tool, I identified two root causes of my resistance: not knowing when the talk was due, and not being clear on the topic of my talk. I decided to create motivation by using my membership's Body Double time later that day to look up the deadline and clarify my topic. This simple step helped me pinpoint how and when I would start.

Make it *YOURS*:

To make the most of the Resistance Busters tool, personalize it to fit the types of tasks and challenges you commonly face. You may want to add or modify the questions under each type of resistance to better reflect your unique experiences. Take note of which strategies are most effective for you. Over time, you'll develop a clearer understanding of what triggers your resistance and how to overcome it, leading to greater productivity and maybe even a bit less stress!

Resistance Busters

Task I'm resisting: _Recording TADD Talk_

What type of resistance do I have?	RESISTANCE BUSTING ?s	My answers	Solutions/Action Steps
Unknowns	What's the first step?	?	List all possible steps from now to done
	How long will this task take?	?	Break it into steps and estimate time for each one
	What don't I know how to do?	N/A	
	Do I need help?	No	
	Who/where can I get help?	N/A	
	What supplies will I need to do it?	N/A	
	What supplies don't I have?	N/A	
	How much will it cost? Can I research/get a quote?	N/A	
	What information do I need before I can start?	Topic clarity	
Low Motivation (I know what to do and how to do it, but don't want to do it!)	What accountability would help me start/finish?	Live Accountability Partnership	Start list of steps during POM Power Hour Body Double session today. Explore topic ideas
	Who can I body double with?	Above	
	Do I need to build in a reward/incentive? What would work for me?	Maybe	See Rewards Menu- pick one during Body Double time (if needed)
	Do I need a deadline/consequence?	?	
	Would taking a walk/getting some exercise/time in nature, help me build up some energy?	No	
	Do I need a snack or a glass of water?	No	
	Can I outsource all or part of it?	No	
Stress and/or Fear	What stress/fears do I have that are making this hard to do? (ex: fear of failure, making a mistake, disappointing someone, etc.)	Not knowing dedline and steps to complete	Look at email and just find deadline! YES!!!
	What's the worst case scenario if I don't do this thing?	Miss opportunity to share information that could positively impact individuals with ADHD	
	What is one "stupid small" thing I can to do to move from where I am now to one step closer to finishing?	Just ID due date for recording submission	Find due date for recording.
	WIFM? (What's In It For Me?) — what will I get from doing it	Sense of accomplishment and a way to connect with people who may not know about my membership community	
What other resistance do I have?			

Patty Blinderman, PCAC, PCC

Resistance Busters

Task I'm resisting: _____

What type of resistance do I have?	RESISTANCE BUSTING ?s	My answers	Solutions/Action Steps
Unknowns	What's the first step?		
	How long will this task take?		
	What don't I know how to do?		
	Do I need help?		
	Who/where can I get help?		
	What supplies will I need to do it?		
	What supplies don't I have?		
	How much will it cost? Can I research/get a quote?		
	What information do I need before I can start?		
Low Motivation (I know what to do and how to do it, but don't want to do it!)	What accountability would help me start/finish?		
	Who can I body double with?		
	Do I need to build in a reward/incentive? What would work for me?		
	Do I need a deadline/consequence?		
	Would taking a walk/getting some exercise/time in nature, help me build up some energy?		
	Do I need a snack or a glass of water?		
	Can I outsource all or part of it?		
Stress and/or Fear	What stress/fears do I have that are making this hard to do? (ex: fear of failure, making a mistake, disappointing someone, etc.)		
	What's the worst case scenario if I don't do this thing?		
	What is one "stupid small" thing I can to do to move from where I am now to one step closer to finishing?		
	WIFM? (What's In It For Me?) — what will I get from doing it		
What other resistance do I have?			

Patty Blinderman, PCAC, PCC

Patty Blinderman, PCAC, PCC

Final Thoughts: Create an ADHD-Friendly Personal Owner's Manual

Create an ADHD-Friendly Personal Owner's Manual (POM) is designed to help individuals with ADHD understand their unique brain wiring and build a personalized guide for managing daily life. By focusing on strengths, developing self-awareness, and using ADHD-friendly tools, this manual offers a comprehensive approach to support the shift from struggling to thriving with ADHD.

Building a Strong Foundation with Successes and Strengths

At the core of a POM is the idea that people with ADHD often focus on their shortcomings and failures, leaving them feeling discouraged and overwhelmed. To counter this, the manual emphasizes the importance of recognizing and celebrating successes and strengths as the foundation for personal growth.

- **Capturing Successes:** The first step in building your POM is capturing successes—whether they're small or large. Successes are essential for building momentum and confidence.
- **Recognizing Strengths:** A list of strengths is just words unless you attach examples and proof of when and where you've used these strengths. The manual encourages you to identify patterns in your successes, building self-awareness around your abilities and creating a positive focus. This serves as the foundation of the POM, helping you to shift your mindset from focusing on struggles and weaknesses to recognizing your strengths and potential.

Executive Function Skills: Understanding Your Brain's Conductor

Understanding **executive function (EF) skills** is a critical component of managing ADHD. The manual provides an overview of these skills, using the models developed by **Dawson and Guare** (Smart but Scattered) and **Dr. Thomas Brown**. Executive functions act as the **brain's conductor**, coordinating essential processes like time management, planning, task initiation, and emotional regulation.

The POM breaks down each EF skill and offers strategies to support areas where ADHD impacts these functions. Knowing which executive function skills are most challenging for you helps create customized strategies for working with your brain, not against it.

Tools for Time Management, Planning, and Prioritizing

Two of the most challenging EF skills for those with ADHD are **time management** and **planning/prioritizing**. In the POM, you'll find ADHD-friendly tools specifically designed to support these skills, such as **monthly, weekly, and daily planners**, as well as creative prioritization tools like the **Stovetop Prioritization Tool** and **Bracket Your Priorities Tool**. These tools allow you to break down overwhelming tasks into manageable steps, helping you stay on track and manage your time effectively.

Task Initiation: Getting Started with the ICNUP Model

Another common challenge for people with ADHD is **task initiation**—starting tasks, especially those that seem tedious or overwhelming. Dr. William Dodson's **ICNUP model** provides a framework to help engage the ADHD brain and make it easier to begin tasks.

The manual includes tools like the **ICNUP Menu, Rewards Menu,** and **To-Do Menu**, designed like a restaurant menu with tasks broken down into manageable parts. This structure allows you to start with small, easy-to-accomplish tasks (appetizers), move on to more significant priorities (main dishes), and enjoy rewards (desserts) for completing your tasks. These tools help build momentum and make task initiation less daunting.

The ADHD-Friendly Toolbox: Tailoring Your Tools for Success

The *ADHD-Friendly Toolbox* chapter emphasizes the importance of customizing tools to fit your unique needs. Each ADHD brain is different, so the POM provides a variety of tools to help you find what works best for you.

Included are the **Tools and Systems Tracker, Sleep Log, Health Visit Log, Tolerations Worksheet,** and **Must Do vs. Might Do Tool**. These are offered to support you to keep track of your most effective strategies, monitor key aspects of your health and well-being, and manage areas of frustration or toleration in your life. This toolbox becomes your go-to resource for handling daily challenges and maintaining routines that work for you.

Growing Self-Awareness: Know Thyself

The final chapter, Know Thyself, is all about fostering self-awareness—understanding your patterns, energy levels, preferences, and needs. By knowing yourself better, you'll be able to make decisions and create systems that align with your strengths rather than constantly battling your weaknesses.

This chapter includes tools such as:
- **Cheat Sheet for Working with Me:** A guide to help others understand how you work best.
- **Top 5 Tolerations Tool:** A way to identify and address the biggest sources of frustration in your life.
- **ADHD Success Puzzle:** A visual representation of your successes, reinforcing positive patterns.
- **Exercise Menu:** A customizable menu of physical activities that align with your energy levels and preferences.
- **Energy Builders and Drainers Tool:** A list of what energizes you and what drains your energy.
- **Resistance Busters:** Questions to help you identify areas of resistance and identify steps to start tasks.

These **Know Thyself** tools help you better understand your ADHD brain and how to work with it, rather than against it. By deepening your self-awareness, you can make choices that support you to struggle less and thrive more!

From Struggle to Thriving: The Power of a Personal Owner's Manual

Create an ADHD-Friendly POM was created to help individuals with ADHD **struggle less and thrive more**. By understanding your strengths, customizing tools to fit your needs, and building a deeper awareness of how you function best, you can shift from frustration and overwhelm to empowerment and success.

Each chapter builds upon the previous one, creating a holistic approach to managing ADHD in a way that is both personal and sustainable. The POM becomes your guide to navigating life with ADHD, helping you stay focused on your strengths, manage challenges, and grow your self-awareness over time.

Remember what Dr. Dodson said, "What works for everyone else doesn't usually work for people with ADHD." This manual provides everything you need to create a customized guide for your life. By focusing on your strengths, identifying your needs, and crafting systems that work for your brain, you can thrive in ways that might have felt out of reach before. This manual is your roadmap to a more empowered, ADHD-friendly life.

Notes

Additional Resources

This list includes a collection of resources to explore for support and guidance in navigating life with ADHD. Please note that some resources listed are available for free while others are books, courses, services, etc, with varying price points.

ADHD-Friendly is not recommending these resources and services. As always, I encourage you to research any resource for yourself in order to decide what is a good fit for what you need, so you can take what works for you and leave the rest behind.

ADHD Support for Adults

- **ADDA (Attention Deficit Disorder Association)**
  Website: add.org
  Provides resources, webinars, and support groups specifically tailored to adults with ADHD.

- **ADHD-Friendly**
  Website: adhdfriendly.com
  Resources include a subscription-based membership community offering live events, on-demand courses, and tools. ADHD-Friendly's shop offers on-demand courses, the ADHD-Friendly Planner, and other tools for purchase. ADHD-Friendly's offerings are focused on tilting the playing field to thrive with ADHD.

- **ADHD-Friendly**
  YouTube Channel: youtube.com/@ADHDFriendly
  Fun and informative weekly videos offering tips and strategies to struggle less and thrive more with ADHD.

- **CHADD (Children and Adults with Attention-Deficit/Hyperactivity Disorder)**
  Website: chadd.org
  Offers support groups, education, and advocacy for people with ADHD of all ages.

- **How to ADHD YouTube Channel**
  Website: youtube.com/HowtoADHD
  Engaging, educational YouTube videos offering tips, tricks, and strategies for living with ADHD.

- **TotallyADD**
  Website: totallyadd.com
  A humorous and insightful resource offering videos, blogs, and tips for living well with ADHD.

ADHD Support for Families and Children

- **ADDitude Magazine**
  Website: additudemag.com
  Offers articles, webinars, and expert advice for managing ADHD in children, teens, and adults.

- **The ADHD Effect on Marriage (Melissa Orlov)**
  Website: adhdmarriage.com
  Offers resources, workshops, and coaching for couples dealing with the impact of ADHD on relationships.

- **CHADD (Children and Adults with Attention-Deficit/Hyperactivity Disorder**
  Website: chadd.org
  Offers support groups, education, and advocacy for people with ADHD of all ages.

- **The Child Mind Institute**
  Website: childmind.org
  Provides research-based resources, articles, and guides for parents of children with ADHD.

- **LD Online**
  Website: ldonline.org
  A helpful site for understanding ADHD in the context of learning disabilities, with resources for children, parents, and teachers.

- **Understood.org**
  Website: understood.org
  A comprehensive resource for parents and educators to support children with ADHD and learning differences.

ADHD Support for Entrepreneurs

- **ADHD for Smart Ass Women with Tracy Otsuka (Podcast)**
  Website: tracyotsuka.com/podcast
  A podcast that offers insights and strategies for high-achieving women, especially entrepreneurs with ADHD.

- **The Faster Than Normal Podcast by Peter Shankman (Podcast)**
  Website: fasterthannormal.com
  A podcast about using ADHD as a superpower, featuring interviews with entrepreneurs and creatives.

Tools and Apps

- **Time Timer**
  Website: https://www.timetimer.com
  The Time Timer is a visual time management tool that can be helpful for individuals with ADHD who struggle with time blindness.

- **The Planner Pad**
  Website: https://plannerpads.com
  The Planner Pad system helps to plan and prioritize by categorizing tasks and funneling them into daily to-dos.

- **Focus@Will**
  Website: https://www.focusatwill.com
  Focus@Will provides music tracks scientifically designed to improve focus and productivity for individuals with ADHD.

- **Forest App**
  Website: https://www.forestapp.cc
  The Forest app gamifies focus by allowing users to grow a virtual tree while staying focused on their work.

- **MindMeister**
  Website: https://www.mindmeister.com
  MindMeister is a mind-mapping tool that helps individuals with ADHD visually organize ideas and projects.

- **Bullet Journal Method**
  Website: https://bulletjournal.com
  The Bullet Journal method offers a flexible and customizable way to manage tasks, goals, and ideas.

- **The Pomodoro Technique**
  Website: https://pomofocus.io
  The Pomodoro Technique is a time management method that breaks work into intervals, typically 25 minutes, followed by a short break.

These resources are offered as a resource for finding support, community, and strategies to help you or your loved ones manage ADHD. Whether you're seeking information for adults, children, families, or entrepreneurs, I hope you find something here to help make the journey more ADHD-friendly.

References

Dawson, P., & Guare, R. (2016).
Smart but Scattered: The Revolutionary "Executive Skills" Approach to Helping Kids Reach Their Potential.
New York: The Guilford Press.
- Information on executive function skills and how they relate to ADHD.

Dodson, W. (n.d.).
"The ICNUP Model for ADHD."
ADDitude Magazine.
- Dr. Dodson's model for task initiation and how it helps engage the ADHD brain.
  Available at: ADDitude Magazine

Brown, T. E. (2006).
Attention Deficit Disorder: The Unfocused Mind in Children and Adults.
New Haven: Yale University Press.
- Dr. Brown's explanation of executive functions as the brain's conductor.

Hallowell, E. M., & Ratey, J. J. (2010).
Driven to Distraction: Recognizing and Coping with Attention Deficit Disorder from Childhood Through Adulthood.
New York: Anchor Books.
- Insights into ADHD management and practical strategies for success.

Neff, K. (2011).
Self-Compassion: The Proven Power of Being Kind to Yourself.
New York: HarperCollins.
- The importance of self-compassion in managing ADHD-related challenges.

ADDitude Magazine. (n.d.).
"ADHD Executive Function and Time Management Skills."
- Articles and insights on managing ADHD, including strategies for time management, planning, and prioritizing.
  Available at: ADDitude Magazine

CHADD (Children and Adults with Attention-Deficit/Hyperactivity Disorder).
"Executive Function: What Is It and How Does ADHD Impact It?"
- Information on how ADHD affects executive functions.
  Available at: chadd.org

www.ingramcontent.com/pod-product-compliance
Lightning Source LLC
Chambersburg PA
CBHW041536120626
46551CB00019B/2720